I0892314

Pillar of Salt

AN AUTOBIOGRAPHY,
WITH 19 EROTIC
SONNETS

♥

Salvador Novo

INTRODUCTION BY
Carlos Monsiváis

TRANSLATED BY
Marguerite Feitlowitz

University of Texas Press
AUSTIN

This project is supported in part by an award from
the National Endowment for the Arts.

ART WORKS.

English translation and "This flower of fourteen petals"
copyright © 2014 by Marguerite Feitlowitz
Sonnets copyright © 2008 by the heirs of Salvador Novo
All rights reserved
Printed in the United States of America
First edition, 2014

Requests for permission to reproduce material from this work should be sent to:
Permissions, University of Texas Press, P.O. Box 7819, Austin, TX 78713-7819
http://utpress.utexas.edu/index.php/rp-form

The paper used in this book meets the minimum requirements of
ANSI/NISO Z39.48-1992 (R1997) (Permanence of Paper). ∞

Design by Lindsay Starr

Library of Congress Cataloging-in-Publication Data
Novo, Salvador, 1904–1974.
[Estatua de sal. English]
Pillar of salt : an autobiography, with 19 erotic sonnets / by Salvador Novo ;
introduction by Carlos Monsiváis ; translated by Marguerite Feitlowitz.
— First edition.
p. cm. — (Texas Pan American Literature in Translation Series)
Includes index.
ISBN 978-0-292-70541-8 (cloth : alk. paper)
1. Novo, Salvador, 1904–1974—Childhood and youth. 2. Authors, Mexican—
20th century—Biography. I. Feitlowitz, Marguerite, translator. II. Title.
PQ7297.N7Z7813 2014
868'.6209—dc23
[B]
2013024216

doi:10.7560/705418

Title page image: *Salvador Novo,* © Colette Urbajtel/Archivo Manuel Álvarez Bravo, SC

Contents

Acknowledgments

To Theresa May, my thanks for instigating this project, and to Casey Kittrell, my gratitude for shepherding it to life. For their early reading of the sonnets, I am grateful to Cola Franzen and David Anderson. For their care, expertise, and unfailing good humor in the preparation of the manuscript, I thank Veronica Jorgensen and Rachel Kelleher.

MARGUERITE FEITLOWITZ

PILLAR OF SALT

INTRODUCTION

The Sidelong World

Where Confession and Proclamation Are Compounded

CARLOS MONSIVÁIS

To Silvia Molloy and Daniel Balderston

HAVING DISCOVERED THE SIDELONG WORLD OF THOSE WHO UNDERSTOOD EACH OTHER WITH A LOOK . . .
Salvador Novo, *Pillar of Salt*

PORTAL

"YOU KNOW, YOU KNOW WHAT I WANT"

In 1945, Salvador Novo (1904–1974) concludes the hundred-and-some pages of his secret autobiography, *Pillar of Salt*, whose title is animated by a double symbolism: the backward look as the most costly of disobediences (curiosity), and citizenship in abhorrent Sodom. Recall the episode (Genesis 19): the inhabitants of the cities of the plain lay siege to two angels sent by Jehovah. Upon seeing such harassment, the Lord decides on the city's destruction, and warns Lot: "Escape for thy life; look not behind thee, neither stay thou in all the plain; escape to the mountain, lest thou be consumed." The rain of fire and brimstone destroys Sodom and Gomorrah, and all the inhabitants and the fruits of the earth. "But his wife looked back from behind him, and she became a pillar of salt."

In his memoirs, Novo is the novelist who will not be held back this time by the urgencies of journalism, he is the re-creator of a most unusual provincial childhood, and he is the forty-year-old gay[1] man trying to impart the highest degree of materiality—that of writing—to the fundamental experience of his life, which is being homosexual. About this last there can be no doubt. If anything defines Novo before the age of sixty, it is his sustained challenge [to convention], his inability to be fake. He has "wagered his heart" on exhibitionism, and imposed himself thanks in part to his qualities: intelligence, abundantly evident talent, irony, self-confidence, industry, and a self-fashioned kind of heroism. From a very young age, he garners both acclaim and denigration, and feeds them both at very high cost. The method by which he "sidesteps our customs" (to quote Jorge Cuesta)[2] is an irritant to machismo and anti-intellectualism, and through his resistance, Novo gets a significant paid advance on freedom, not only in terms of sexual preference but also in appearance. In an environment defined by barbarism, how does he survive his own mannerisms; his habit of wearing makeup; sweet, soft voice; plucked eyebrows; and, later, the colossal rings and variety of wigs? (Questioned on the subject of his toupee, Novo replies: "Wearing the toupee is the toupee.")

Before he gained undeniable recognition, nothing so stimulated Novo as his condition of exile from respectability. In an interview with Emmanuel Carballo (in *Diecinueve protagonistas de la literature mexicana* [Nineteen Protagonists of Mexican Literature[3]]), he is very clear [in his reference to a prominent homosexual literary figure]:

> . . . "Jaime [Torres Bodet] hasn't had a life, from the time he was young he has had a biography."
>
> "And you?"
>
> "I, on the contrary, have had a life. The biography of a man like me would do injury to 'respectable customs.'"

Much of Novo's work and behavior revolves around his sexual transgression: the poems of a desolated outcast, the autobiographical transvestitism of *Romance de Angelillo y Adela*, the epigrams, the poems in which he abominates his own body and exalts in self-directed sarcasm, *Pillar of Salt*, the brief theatrical piece *El tercer Fausto* [The Third Faust], the cultivation of a provocative dandyism, the exaltation of the pose in the very niche of an identity never to be forsaken. Without beating about the bush, in Novo homosexuality is the primordial impulse, stimulant, and sign of his identity.

In 1945, Novo is already well beyond the period described in *Pillar of Salt*. He has published fundamental books (*Ensayos* [Essays, several volumes], *XX Poemas* [1925], *Return Ticket* [original title of Novo's account of his trip to Hawaii, 1928], *Espejo* [Mirror; poems,

1933], *Nuevo amor* [New Love; poems, 1933]), is one of the great journalistic innovators, has survived the campaign of attacks and ridicule of the 1930s, and has renounced any and all love relationships. While the period [of the mid-1940s] withholds its maximum respect and even excessively censures him, the moral lynching he suffers typically takes the form of rumors and jokes, and Novo also has an admiring circle, earns significantly more money, and, perhaps because of this, attenuates the belligerence he once lavished on his sonnets and satiric verses. So, then, why write *Pillar of Salt*? Why be the only one in this whole long period to unveil his strictly forbidden private life? Of course, the text was not intended for immediate release, nor in 1945 could such a licentious publisher be found, although Novo had already published, in 1936, *El tercer Fausto* and, in 1944, *Dueño mío* [My Lord and Master], the collection of four love sonnets. What is evident is the urgency to record on paper that which was ferociously hidden or blurred or unnameable, to demonstrate the audacity that gives meaning to his existence. I remember in 1965, in the homes of both Emmanuel Carballo and Don Rafael Giménez Siles,[4] Maese Novo reading an excerpt from *Pillar of Salt*, the publication of which he was unsure of. Let me note Novo's elation at the astonishment he caused.

I

"THAT ISN'T SPOKEN OF IN MY HOUSE!"

How to explain that nineteenth-century Mexico had no laws or regulations pertaining to sexual minorities, no articles, books, literary characters, or even caricaturized representations of gay people? In Europe and the United States the situation was very different. We are informed by Jeffrey Weeks in *Sexuality and Its Discontents* that, between 1898 and 1908, close to a thousand books on homosexuality were published in Europe. And in Europe and North America, between 1880 and the First World War, free love, abortion, masturbation, homosexuality, prostitution, obscenity, and sex education were topics for discussion, at least among enlightened minorities. In the very Catholic nation of Mexico, however, the only one of those subjects mentioned, to instructive and sermonizing ends, is prostitution. (There are more references to masturbation in the catechisms of the eighteenth century than in all of the nineteenth.)

Occult logic: that which has no name does not exist, and this sordid nothing is filtered, with great contempt, in conversation. If during the viceroyalty sodomites were condemned to burn at the stake because they "had transmuted the natural order," in the nineteenth century they are never alluded to in writing, in accordance with the proven tactic: scant detail about sin lets innocence shine more brightly. If there is no illuminating scandal, there is no category for suspicion. If the abomination is inconceivable, who can foster suspicion? Consider the youthful episode that Guillermo Prieto refers to in *Memorias de mis tiempos* [Memories of My Times; 1923]. In this ardent text, nineteen-year-old Prieto criticizes the president of the Republic, Anastasio Bustamante,[5] who soon afterward called him in:

> "So what's new, man?" he says, "What's going on?"
>
> "I come at the request of Your Excellency."
>
> "Let's see, my friend . . ." (after examining me for a good moment). "Do you really believe me to be that ruler who is cruel and negligent of public instruction?"
>
> I kept silent; but I was wary . . .

In the conversation that follows, Prieto tells Bustamante about his amorous triumphs and defeats, which they enjoy like two high school boys sharing provocative secrets.

> "So," he said, "do you still consider me that Minotaur the newspapers go on about?"

And without waiting for an answer, he shouted, "López! López!" (López came).

This López, his intimate assistant, was a huge, lean black man with kinky hair.

"Put a bed in my room for the gentleman, obey him, and make it known you'll obey him because he is like my son" (I listened astonished).

From adversary to *room mate*[6] in a single day. Prieto and his nineteenth-century readers find it very normal that all of a sudden, and for no other reason than that he is brilliant and ingenuous, a very young man moves in to the presidential bedroom. The attitude is irreproachable, because no one would think of any other interpretation, nor would it make sense to suggest one. Freudian suspicions were a long way off, and not until the mid-twentieth century would homosexuality in Mexico be considered—or wish to be considered—from a scientific perspective. Until then, Mexico was constructing its national selfhood, implanting norms that combined Catholic traditions with a new and ample catalogue of civic virtues. Society considered a predilection for one's own sex as so remote and abject that there was no need to stress the contrast with the psychological and corporeal virtues of virility. Therefore *the heinous sin* so completely contradicts the "essence" of Mexicans (and of human beings) that it is left to oral culture to punish "faggots," those monopolists of affronts against masculinity.

The first public acknowledgment of these moral transgressors happens in 1901, with the police scandal of the Dance of the Forty-one. However incredible it may seem, before that there had only been fleeting and joking mentions of "repugnant little youths." In England, the trials of Oscar Wilde (1895) suddenly bring to light the networks of "wayward" youths and their meeting places, and frame the pathetic, timid, and magnificent defense of "the love that dare not say its name"; in Mexico, as soon as the roundup of the Forty-one in the capital signals a break with the prohibitions of traditionalism, of that "hatred that dare not write the name of the hated," a number, 41, became for nearly a century, a joke. Despite the resonances of the event, very little is known about the actual dance: on November 20, 1901, on Calle de la Paz, the police interrupt a dance being held by homosexuals, transvestites, and descendants of the notable families of the *porfiriato*.[7] Instantly, the roundup acquires a legendary profile: the majority of the detainees are sent to Yucatán to do forced labor, and, according to the never-refuted popular rumor, one of those present, who was immediately let go, is Ignacio de la Torre, Porfirio Díaz's son-in-law. Some flee over the rooftops, others buy their freedom, and the rest sweep the streets on their way to the railroad station. In a series of prints, José Guadalupe Posada establishes the popular image of the event, imagined as a fiesta of "phenomena," of gentlemen clumsily cross-dressed, with mustaches and sideburns, mixing it up with low-class homosexuals in a merry dance toward scandal. "Here we see the nancy boys / Such pretty little fancy boys" is the title of one of the prints, and an accompanying verse gives a festive account of "the great singular dance":

> Forty-one dandies
> half of them disguised
> as sweet young women,
> dancing with abandon.
> The other half in suits
> befitting men,
> dipping and twirling
> the *flaming little faggots*.

In 1902 come the arrests of two homosexuals, "Lady Mustaches" and "He of the Two Carnations," who are both sent to forced labor. That year, the Moriones sisters, theater producers, celebrate the one-hundredth performance of Perrín and Palacios's zarzuela *Enseñanza libre*,[8] with the "roles reversed," actors playing actresses and vice versa, something common in Mexico since the middle of the nineteenth century, according to Luis Reyes de la Maza in his *Circo, maroma y teatro (1810–1910)* [Circus, Acrobatics, and Theater].[9] But machismo is also a cultural invention, and journalists, very aware of the custom of "reversed roles," cry out in surprise, calling the production "repugnant," and denigrating the producers, "who are already rehearsing a zarzuela with Mexican actors called *The Forty-one*."

Public scandal is the only way to accept that homosexuals exist. The Señoras Moriones defend themselves: the one-hundredth performances of comedies have always been celebrated in this manner, without any protest, and in fact they are not working on a zarzuela with that "infamous" title. (From then on and until very recently in popular culture, the *gay* is a transvestite and there is only one species of homosexual: the effeminate.) In an unusual book, *Los cuarenta y uno: Novela crítico-social* [The Forty-one: A Social Criticism Novel] (1906), the author, Eduardo A. Castrejón, took the usual tack of preaching against homosexuality as "a grave insult to Nature," and describes an abominable evening:

> The degenerate hearts of those young aristocrat prostitutes palpitated in that immense bacchanal.
>
> The boundless happiness at having female clothing on their bodies, the womanly postures, the carnivalesque voices, the lavatory–dressing room all made for a chamber of the fantastic; the many perfumes, the embraces, the loud and feverish kisses, represented the degrading images of Sodom and Gomorrah, of the orgiastic feasts of Tiberius, of Commodius and Caligula, where the explosive fire of savage passion devoured the flesh, consuming it in the desires for the most unbridled prostitution.

For Castrejón there is no doubt: these are "inflamed, shameful, loathsome youths in terms of the future and for all generations, [they are] the dregs of society, the dereliction of honorable masculinity that adores women for their specifically female attributes of beauty." In the novel, Ignacio de la Torre is [represented by] Don

Pedro Marruecos, the center of that perverted society, and the only one who escapes from the party, whose igneous moment amazes Castrejón:

> Meanwhile, enthusiasm was building in the room. Phosphorescent eyes, lewd eyes, languid eyes; undulating prosthetic hips, with all the grace of their irreproachable curves; powdered faces, plastered with makeup; wigs marvelously adorned with combs encrusted with gold and the finest jewels; calves chiseled with tight cotton wrappings, looking genuinely, unmuscularly slender; enormous, prominent prosthetic breasts straining to escape their prison; grotesque expressions and fake voices; the combination of it all rendered the orgy rather macabre and fantastic.

Then comes the fall, the shame, the crowd watching with pleasure as the Forty-one leave for the Yucatán for an infernal life of forced labor.

> How laughable it was to see the grotesque picture of the fashionable Forty-one, raising a shovel and striking with the pickax, sweating, squalid, and most of the time crying their eyes out.
>
> The soldiers taunted them without respite every day, with pretend voices:
>
> "And where are you going in your lovely party dress?"
>
> "Darling, don't work so hard, it'll ruin your figure!"
>
> "Are you suffocating, my lovely? Then use your fan!"

One of the soldiers' songs becomes popular when a newspaper in the capital published it:

> Look at me, here I go, boy,
> fitted out for the Yucatán
> I'm part of a convoy
> dancing jigs and cancan.

After the episode of the Forty-one, secrecy concerning the subject is maintained. There are no reports on the meeting places or habits of those who were arrested, and their identities, though not disclosed, are intuited (thinking of themselves in the context of a certain tradition, they accept that that tradition totally condemns them, and they consider themselves monstrous beings, aberrations of Nature). In spite of all this, the main barrier begins to crumble—that of the silence in writing. Rob Buffington, in "*Los jotos*: Contested Visions of Homosexuality in Modern Mexico" (in *Sex and Sexuality in Latin America*, edited by Daniel Balderston and Donna J. Guy, New York University Press, 1997), calls attention to *Los criminales en México* (Tipografía El Fénix, 1904) by Carlos Roumagnac, criminalist, journalist, and man of letters during the time of Porfirio Díaz. Roumagnac describes his research at the Belén prison and at the new Federal Penitentiary in the capital. The director of the prison tries to isolate all "known pederasts," in order to put an end to the "bloody fights" among jealous inmates, and in response, those who had been singled out parade before the other prisoners "without shame or shyness, but rather, ostentatiously displaying their feminine voices and mannerisms."

"WILDE IS DESTINED TO BE POPULAR AMONG US"

Elsewhere, Wilde's trials are already being mentioned. Finally, in 1913, in the *Revista de Revistas* [Review of Reviews], the writer Julio Torri analyzes the proceedings (the text is included in *El diálogo de los libros* [Dialogue of the Books] (Fondo de Cultura Económica, 1980). Torri is ahead of his time, opposing those who "crudely pursue any idea or line of thought of a scientific or artistic nature that runs contrary to the stability of the family and the State," and he ridicules the French committee urging the mutilation of Wilde's tomb in the Parisian cemetery of Père-Lachaise:

> No one is surprised at the savage persecution of everything Wilde represents; a disgraceful army beyond number has sworn war to the death against a writer, a poet, and to the degree that it concerns them, because his life was not totally edifying in the way that would suit the most ignorant and contemptible members of any Anglican congregation.

In 1913 it was highly unusual to defend Wilde, and even more surprising was the mockery of charges against him, arising from the "flock of mediocre, philistine, and semicultured people." Torri concludes:

> The day is not far off when we will turn our face to Wilde with a generous smile, and it will seem to us that the terrible catastrophe of his life has the prestige of martyrdom. His mania to *épater* and his waywardness will make us smile in the same way we smile at Wordsworth's petulance, De Quincey's attitude, Lamb's affinity for gin with water . . .

Torri is consistent. In the October 1, 1916, issue of *Revista de Revistas*, he praises Wilde profusely:

> The dandyism of our young men of letters wearing flowery "boutonnieres" as well as the *caballeras* [feminine gentlemen] of floating curls is a more than eloquent indication. Wilde is destined to be popular among us. His influence will attenuate the habitual narrowness of our judgment, lighten our heavy spirit, and renew the stuffy, unbreathable atmosphere in which our intellectuals languidly bloom.

Wilde, the culture's oxygen. In the years of armed struggle, Torri's humanism is truly exceptional.

. . . .

II

"As though we were rubbish / and the whirlwind swept us away"

What explains the emergence in the decade of the twenties of a small sector of artists and writers who, without any warning, live their sexual option more or less "in the open"? Or, put another way, what provokes *the visibility* of gays, that partial but very effective confrontation of the taboo? This *appearance of the moral underground* can be explained by cultural factors (the circulation of Freud's ideas, the end of the country's informational isolation, changes in international literature, etc.), but above all by the outbreak of the Mexican Revolution, the other name for a group of phenomena ranging from anticlericalism and secularism to the battles and factions, to the vital explosion in the capital of the Republic.

In Mexico, the nineteenth century fomented—predictably and jubilantly—hypocrisy, ignorance, sexual phobia, the ubiquitous and exhausting moralist preachings that all came together in a kind of civilizing pact. (Consider the hundreds of Catechisms that vaunt the generosity of the Counter-Reformation.) It falls to the Revolution to give the fatal blow to such a structure of guilt-inducing silences, along with the masses who are forcefully mobilizing and señoritas who, at least for a few hours, are losing their virginity. Cities taken over by the Revolution, massive migrations, legions of children without fathers, and waves of prostitutes make the realities of desire impossible to hide. One way of putting it is that the Revolution, with its temporary demolition of modesty, somehow "sexualizes" the country, making it possible for these corporeal realities to rise to the surface in comic theaters; makes fun of *the arch-dignified silences* around carnality; calls attention to the "social conquest" in the mixing of high-ranking officers with prostitutes; gives notice that single mothers (who usually emigrate from small villages) are the new national institution. Above all, the Revolution weakens the absolute sway of moral prohibitions. This "sexualizing" of Mexico, while to a degree that today we consider conservative, disrupts tyrannical notions. Finally, "if I am to be killed tomorrow, let me just sin right now."

The Revolution is also, and most especially, social energy, the vigor that infuses exploits on the symbolic fields of battle. If Don Porfirio—emblem of the immovable—has fallen, why not rhymed poetry, academic painting, the naturalistic novel, a society that is closed and punitive? With the collapse of the dictatorship, with the enthronement for a few years of relative morality (the imminence of death quickly modifies customs), a new sensibility filters in that while still very much in debt to an earlier age, is already capable of committing numerous "sacrileges" that don't ultimately quite rise to the name. This is why, among the consequences of the Revolution, we can also find the certainty among very ample sectors of the population that the suppression of intimacy is outrageous and pointless, that there is little reason to panic at What Will They Say, that it is absurd to renounce desire in favor of "Respectability" with all its anxieties. In a single decade the semifeudal notions of Decency that were harbored in villages and resided in cities are pulverized. And the Revolution also, by eliminating a great number of conventions, which we could group under the rubric "I don't want to know myself what I do at night," gives fluidity to secularization. *Machista* prohibitions and reactions remain in place, but there is already a questioning of the anachronism of the system that polices consciences and instills feelings of guilt. The process is by no means universal, but in the capital its vigor consolidates spaces of tolerance. Pretensions of supreme decency persist, but they are more and more the result of a social pact and not of immovable convictions. Prejudice moves elsewhere.

In its version of the caudillo temperament, nationalist art and literature, and the theory of [national] singularity, the Mexican Revolution never excessively anchors itself in the ideal of the New Man, which in the Soviet Revolution leads to concentration camps, and in the Cuban Revolution to forced labor for homosexuals, Jehovah's

Witnesses, and "antisocials." In Mexico, the calls for a New Man are highly declamatory, transferring to the civil arena an idealization of the military: bravery (no longer suicidal), daring, faith in the People, untainted masculinity, contempt for weakness or softness. The Olympus of Strong Men is transmuted into a national, nationalist, and industrial myth: "all *macho* all the time," with resonances that even today are so costly and tragic. This play with patriarchy is, of course, stage setting that tries to mask a society devastated by alcoholism, domestic violence, lethal street fighting, misogynist abuse, rape as "every man's *droit du seigneur*." The Mexican Revolution's cult of machismo has among its consequences—while not the most primary, it is not the least injurious—the gloating persecution of difference and the unanimous forgetting of the human rights of gays. Not a single protest is raised against the wicked imprisonment of "faggots," whose only crime is their sexual preference; no one worries about the savage crimes committed *against*—rather than *by*—homosexuals. What would be the point? Homosexuals are not human, let alone compatriots (in that "lofty" version of what constitutes humanity).

For those living the Revolution, the war takes on the imperatives of worship, among them, the singular, redundant version of virility. And so when that quintessential revolutionary Emiliano Zapata learns about the homosexuality of Manuel Palafox, his ideologue and redactor of numerous documents, he is so infuriated that it is only through the power of political argument that he is obliged to pardon Palafox. (After the death by firing squad of Otilio Montaño, another internal liquidation would have been disastrous for Zapatism.) But in urban areas, reactions are not so extreme. In his *Memorias* (published by Editorial Grijalbo, 1982), Gonzalo N. Santos, arbiter of the revolutionary picaresque, recounts a typical incident: President Emilio Portes Gil[10] is complaining to the parliamentarians of the lower houses that the Treasury isn't giving him money. The argument goes like this: "Fine, but the president of the Republic has an enormous budget and discretionary funds, in addition to his salary." The president of the Republic responds: "The entire budget was slashed by that faggot bastard Montes de Oca" (Luis, Secretary to the Treasury). Santos, then in the lower house, continues:

> This Montes de Oca was a kid, almost a dwarf, and indeed a famous faggot, and when in Chambers he would raise objections to our budgets, we would turn to the influential Chicho (diminutive of Narciso, because Big Narciso was our nickname for Representative Ezequiel Padilla, who became Minister of Foreign Affairs during General Ávila Camacho's presidency . . . but I must clarify that Ezequiel Padilla was never a *faggot*, only in love with his own presence, and the other so-called Chicho or Narciso Two, as we also called him, was more full of himself than Padilla; drove a very elegant, convertible; wore gloves; and paraded himself every day along Avenida Madero, the Zócalo, and Cinco de Mayo, where everyone strolled in those days). So we would recur to Montes de Oca, which is to say, at this representative who was said to be the Minister of the Treasury's lover. "Go see your girlfriend and if he doesn't sign our budget, I'll yank out your teeth." He would laugh and tell me, "Don't worry, boss," and would invariably return with the Chamber's budget, signed by Montes de Oca.

The eccentric Luis Montes de Oca, a Colonial art collector, is the object of general scorn, including that of the president of the Republic, for comitting crimes against the species. And if a man whose high position guarantees him significant privileges can be subjected to public ridicule, what can be expected for those effeminate men with high voices, men who were discreet but did not go unnoticed, prisoners and those who had been blackmailed by the police, men who fled their villages in order to save their lives?

"Effeminates" of the poorer classes—simply because of their appearance—were subjected to serial humiliations, stripped of all recognizable humanity, and only then allowed to survive. These are the men who are jailed for "moral failings and violations of respectable customs" (the most typical are the ones sent to the special "J" section of the Palacio de Lecumberri prison); they are the faggots [*los jotos*] on display at the San Marcos Fair in Aguascalientes; they are the effeminate boys in the Tehuantepec Isthmus raised by their families as women (called *berdaches* in Zapotec). In the capital, homosexuals with resources, talent, ingenuity, audacity, money, and social relationships get the concession of a "moral dispensation," which, without totally isolating them, never offers full integration, not even in the case of the most highly respected Carlos Pellicer, whose sexuality, while never obvious, was always known. And though the law does not prohibit consensual homosexuality among adults, society exacts a high price for the transgression.

In no period is it easy to transgress the ultimate prohibitions of myth and custom, even if it is legal and legitimate, but in the era of undefeated *machismo*, the payment for the sin is death (physical and social). According to rigid classifications, until recently there were only two types of homosexuals in Mexico: the faggot of sandwich stands and bordellos, and the society fairy. The rest are fleeting shadows, who, while lacking a pigeonhole, are surrounded by malevolent rumor or always treated with condescension and diminutives ("Juanito / Robertito"), underscoring the enduring infantilizing of those outside of the maturity of marriage. Few escape harassment. The artist Chucho Reyes Ferreira is expelled from Guadalajara as one of many "deviants" of the time, and forced to sweep the streets on the way to the train that will remove him from the city as crowds watch and cheer; the Colima police pursue the artist Alfonso Michel as a vicious delinquent; two homosexuals from Guadalajara's "High Society," Guillermo Hermosillo and Gabriel Orendáin—Guille and Gaby—are made the subjects of a silly cheer that could still be heard at sporting events in the 1950s:

Here's to Guillé, here's to Gabe
Here's to "Oh Yes . . . Honey!" What a babe!
Go [Team name]
Ohhh God . . . What a babe . . .

A notable case is that of the extraordinary painter Alfonso Michel, very well documented by Jorge Chávez Carrillo (*Alfonso Michel: Mito, leyenda* [Myth, Legend], Universidad de Colima, 1993). Until the 1950s, chain gangs known as *cuerdas* (groups of prisoners sent to the penal colony at Islas Marías, among whom were homosexuals rounded up by chance) were frequent. In 1932, it is decided that a *cuerda* will be rounded up in Manzanillo, and Michel, also called Chopín, is in danger:

> La Gallina [The Hen] recognized the "messenger" standing in the door. "Marentes sent me." El Feo [The Ugly One] grabs him: "What's going on?"
>
> "At six the *cuerda* will arrive, the train is on time . . . so you know, it is up to you." He received a peso in exchange for the news and went on his way to alert others and collect for the warning. El Feo ran to find Alfonso but didn't find him, in the brothel or anywhere else.
>
> El Feo went to find Severo. "Find Chopín and grab him by the balls and hide him . . ." Chopín spent the night at Audiencia beach, led at gunpoint to a solitary and isolated dwelling by Severo Lezama, a thug for hire who owed El Feo his life . . .
>
> In the evening, the soldiers from the garrison in the square and the sailors stationed in the port where the maneuvers would take place all mobilized to reassure the population during the embarkation of the convicts, criminals, and thieves who were sentenced to prison on the Islas Marías.
>
> The announcement was made that faggots would be imprisoned and exiled as a social prophylaxis, and added to the chain gang, so that it would be said that the government was moral, and also because blackmail, hiding and helping suspects to flee, could be exchanged for large sums of money or jewels. Jorge Michel was in Colima, with business at the State Government Palace; right there a messenger stopped him with the threatening news. Chopín was in no danger in Colima provided that he pay for the warning.

At the Manzanillo port, a police squad surrounded the Pedregosa area in search of "Pola Negri."[11] The secret police happened upon the *Garrobo* [male] iguana who was the *puto*'s ["the whore" Negri's] lover; amidst orders and shouts and insults to their mothers, they attacked. One of the secret policemen bent over, wounded by the *Garrobo*'s dagger. In the struggle, they riddled him with bullets, [and] "Pola Negri," tied up, howled like a wounded beast. The bordello's doorman, Don Blas, was found dead the next morning of natural causes, stiff with fright. This roundup completed the quota. That night, the handcuffed homosexuals onboard kept a vigil until dawn, hoping for a miracle. The naval ship raised anchor. They say that "Pola Negri" died on the high seas.

Severo Lezama delivered Chopín at seven in the morning, frightened but safe and sound. La Gallina gave him tea to calm his panic and lunch to help him sleep.

"THOSE OF DUBIOUS PSYCHOLOGICAL CONDITION"

In the twenties and thirties, those of a certain cultural tendency, the group that takes its name from the magazine *Contemporáneos* (Novo, [Xavier] Villaurrutia, Jaime Torres Bodet, Jorge Cuesta, Bernardo Ortiz de Montellano, Gilberto Owen, José Gorostiza, Enrique González Rojo) are ultimately marginal because even though they work in the official bureaucracy, the culture that is important to them comes as a surprise to the country, and because they constitute a circle with broad critical judgment on the subject of behaviors. Only some of them are homosexuals, but defamation admits no exceptions. The part for the whole, and "hurrah!" for the opportunity to destroy enemies with such vulnerable flanks. Even Alfonso Reyes upon his return to Mexico is astonished and confides to his friend Antonio G. Solalinde (August 25, 1924): "I always believe that the young are right. There is a great deal of faggotry [*mariconería*] among them, a new sickness here, and that distances me from many of them and causes me to suffer, as I am not as skeptical and indifferent as I had thought myself to be." The *new sickness*[12] is disturbing enough to cause organized exasperation. Recall what the estridentista poet Manuel Maples Arce[13] said in his memoirs (*Soberana juventud* [Sovereign Youth], 1967):

> On one occasion we met in the Green Room at the Chamber of Deputies to discuss the problem of homosexuals in theater, art, and literature. Although there were disapproving statements, the devil put his finger in and *they* [the homosexuals present] remained more self-satisfied than ever, while people wondered aloud why *they* were allowed to move about so freely, when in the time of Porfirio Díaz they had been made to sweep the streets, as happened to those who made the number 41 so famous that it was popularized in a print by Posada. Public morality does not depend on a [single] group; it is, as [José] Ortega y Gasset would say, the style of a society, and if that [society] should accept that each individual make his own judgments with the ease of flying a kite, then there is no possibility of dignifying [those judgments and that society].
>
> Their preponderance was due to a mafia mindset. At times they truly persecuted those who resisted joining their attempts to establish intellectual hegemony or who refused to enter into that scheme. It was the period of unrelenting publicity for Proust and Gide, whose works provided a home for faggots with all their dramas, and for the cynicism of pederasts.
>
> In order to escape all responsibility, they adopted a position of neutrality that allowed them to survive above all the ideological conflicts that have beset the Mexican nation. They were never on the right or on the left . . . They held to an aesthetic that absolved them of commitment and put them on the margin of any responsible obligation.
>
> In the shadow of protectors who wanted to be seen as intellectual Maecenas, they published, with the nation's money, an anthology in which the favored ones wrote their panegyrics, singing each other's praises.

The law of least resistance. Those who were excluded from or not sufficiently praised in the *Antología de la poesía mexicana [moderna]* [Anthology of Modern Mexican Poetry] (1928), a group effort under the direction of Jorge Cuesta, disqualify their critics for "moral" reasons. Once again, a macho strategy comes into play, which, under the pretext offered by "the little weirdos" [*los raritos*], praises its own poetic work, its revolutionary nature, its commitment, its independence from protectors, and its unblemished virility. Basically, Maples Arce's protest is a great act of self-praise based on disdain for "the faggots' mafia." Why were all these deviants treating a poet as great as Maples like dirt?

The campaign against homosexuals is very intense. Orozco caricatures them (*Los Anales*); and in the murals Diego Rivera made for the Ministry of Public Education, he mocks cultural Maecenas Antonieta Rivas Mercado with a depiction of an energetic revolutionary woman handing her a broom with which Rivas is to sweep from the palette of a lifeless painter the vestiges of the abominable symbolism of white roses and a 1928 issue of *Contemporáneos*. With a desolate expression, Rivas Mercado watches a male revolutionary worker tripping a male poet who has the ears of an ass. Years later, in his painting *The Forty-one*, Antonio Ruiz el Corzo[14] selects his elitist scoundrels: Novo, Villaurrutia, [painters] Roberto Montenegro and Lupe Marín, as well as Antonieta Rivas Mercado.

The moral lynching has vast cultural and literary resonances. At that time, the criticism of homosexuals as a sexual category belongs without a doubt to a social construct that depends, in great measure, on conceding only a negligible space to women. According to the guardians of the Norm, a homosexual voluntarily degrades himself by resembling women, and the *machista* condemnation is both the public and private expression against such debasement. The *joto* [faggot] threatens the continuation of the species and of fundamental values, and this insult becomes extreme when it can be seen, where before its invisibility had rendered it nonexistent. How is it possible that a deviant so deserving of scorn should not be imprisoned or annihilated, and can't they all simply be sent to gather dust down in the catacombs or be shipped as slave labor to the Valle Nacional?[15] Persecution, disguised as loyalty to tradition, intensifies. In 1925, Jiménez Rueda[16] complains about the "feminization of literature," and it's necessary to remind him of the existence of Mariano Azuela's *The Underdogs* (*Los de abajo*)[17] in order to dissuade him of his lamentations for lost virility. In 1930, the revolutionary painters of the ¡30-30! group demand the resignation of various government officials, including those who are "dubious":

> And we are against homosexuality, an imitation of today's French bourgeoisie, and between them—who now are favored—and us tireless fighters, there exists the chasm of our honesty, which will not be sold for a position. The government must not maintain in its ministries those of dubious psychological condition.

Complaint leads to direct action. A Committee for Public Health is established in the Chamber of Deputies to "purge the government of counterrevolutionaries," and on October 31, 1934, a group of intellectuals (José Rubén Romero, Mauricio Magdaleno, Rafael F. Muñoz, Mariano Silva y Aceves, Renato Leduc, Juan O'Gorman, Xavier Icaza, Francisco L. Urquizo, Emilio Abreu Gómez, Humberto Tejero, Jesús Silva Herzog, Héctor Pérez Martínez, and Julio Jiménez Rueda) asks this Committee that if it is trying to purify public administration,

> it should make its agreements extensively known among the individuals of dubious morality who hold official positions and those who, through their effeminate behaviors, in addition to constituting a punishable example, create an atmosphere of corruption that reaches such an extreme that it impedes the implantation of virile virtues in young men [. . .] If the presence of the fanatic, of the reactionary, is being combated in public offices, then the presence of the hermaphrodite incapable of identifying with the workers engaged in social reform must also be combated.

The guardians of this nationalism (among them, novelists of the Mexican Revolution, poets, painters, and government officials) want to eliminate such agents of weakness from the fabric of the nation in a single "Night of the Long Knives" waged on behalf of the budget and respectability. Cultural nationalism is the implacable enemy that, with its theory of racial virtue, provides a "theoretical foundation" to its active intolerance of that which is "other." This is why the subject of homosexuality, even though it covers one aspect of *Contemporáneos* but does not reach the level of a literary criterion, serves the opposite function of capturing certain manifestations of social psychology. Orthodoxy converts the heterodox into a favorite target, but among those harassed, the effort to skirt the norm produces novel aesthetic practices and expressions in the search for authenticity.

III

"ALL ON TOP OF EACH OTHER"

It is better to marry than to burn, affirms Saint Paul the Apostle. But already in the decade of the twenties, especially in Mexico City, a significant number of homosexuals accentuate their behavior: it is better to sacrifice prestige than to repress desire, it is better to emblematize the "betrayal of one's sex," defaming along the way the National Essence, than to renounce instinct. And in the bohemian bourgeoisie, at the start of the institutional phase of the Revolution, there were those who assumed their sexual dissidence with all possible discretion and tranquillity. They are politicians (Luis Montes de Oca, Treasury Secretary under Plutarco Elías Calles, and Genaro Estrada, Foreign Relations Secretary), writers (Salvador Novo, Xavier Villaurrutia, Carlos Pellicer, Elías Nandino), painters (Roberto Montenegro, Manuel Rodríguez Lozano, Abraham Ángel, Alfonso Michel, Chucho Reyes Ferreira, Agustín Lazo,

Enrique Asúnsulo), film producers (Felipe Subervielle, Agustín J. Fink), theater people and actors (the most famous, and one who emigrated, Ramón Novarro), singers (José Mojica), popular composers (Gabriel Ruiz, Pepe Guízar).

On the evidence of this movement, which is encouraged by the growing number of secular environments, we see taking shape, even if only on the margins, the universe of different [that is to say, homosexual] desire, or *deseo distinto*. God has not died, but He no longer has time to keep track of everything, and also, on a more earthly plane, Mexico's cultural isolation and absolute dependence on a single civilizing model (that of France) come to an end. In addition, violence has granted an opening to such a range of attitudes that, among those most anxious for Progress, one more doesn't so much matter. To use an expression of the time: "If God already knows, let men know too." And if liberated women, atheists, priest-bashers, communists, proselytizers for free love all let themselves be seen, why not—in spite of everything—gays? (Lesbians go unperceived, and it would be some time before they and bisexuals could be situated, or granted their place. The most common is the existence of men whose masculinity was said to have "slipped" or lapsed.) Heretics circulate in a territory of minimal tolerance—though in comparative terms, even the still revolutionary capital could be considered "maximally" tolerant—though of course they are made to pay with a quota of marginalization, aggressions, teasing, gossip, jokes. Withal, the "traitors to Nature" do not desist from their behavior, making it more or less patent, so that what before had been sexually unthinkable is no longer so, and this, together with the possibility of creating scandal, results in a *de facto* liberation.

Those who form the cultural vanguard are pressured to break with the isolation that has characterized Mexico since independence, for an urgent catching-up with what is happening in the metropoli of the world, to bring to the country (especially to the capital) the experiences of modernity. In order to cast off the double oppression of traditionalism and chauvinism, outdated prejudices and canons need to be destroyed, rhymed poetry must be renounced, painting must be conscious of Picasso, and gays, most especially, must assume André Gide's dictum: "Live Dangerously!" which is to say, live in a way that challenges social narrow-mindedness. The poet Xavier Villaurrutia shares the credo of his generation with a journalist named Ortega at the *Revista de Revistas* (April 10, 1932):

> It is Gide's morality that interests us, that interests me. Humane, profound, brave, it helps one live. Become who you are, said Nietzsche. Live as who you are, André Gide seems to be saying.
>
> You know, our familiarity with the moral oeuvre of Gide arises from the coincidence that we too are part of a moment characterized by a new spirit, so his work resonates for us as a confrontation with moral hypocrisy. Before Gide, it seemed absurd to talk about oneself, to show oneself as one is.

To show oneself as one is. To make literary counsel into a program for the edification of the dissident personality. The power of the poetic (and *living dangerously* is poetic action, according to Gide's followers) is akin to the existential and cultural power of a handful of men *coming out*.[18]

"A PROUST WHO LIVES IN MEXICO!"

Among the heretics, no one is more openly scandalous than Salvador Novo, or more utilized by the promoters of the Virile Fatherland, both for his powers of provocation and as an opportunity to finger notable dissidents as part of their heterosexual blockade.

But if the harassment and demonization are inclement, the degree to which Novo employs them creates the legend that will become both his *via crucis* and his glory. For him, provocation becomes an instrument of mental health. Everything shows this to be so—his relations with truckers, wrestlers, and bus drivers, and chauffeurs, with workers, with soldiers, and this, leaving nothing to doubt, balances obviousness with bravery. Here is how he is seen during those years: Manuel Rodríguez Lozano paints him in a taxi, wearing a dressing gown, while swirling all around him his pick-up city becomes phantasmagorical. Tina Modotti portrays him as haughty, disdainful; and Manuel Álvarez Bravo captures him in his magnificent arrogance, daring the viewer to reject him. In June of 1938, *Rotofoto*, headed by José Pagés Llergo, publishes a series of photos of Novo, Montenegro, and the singer José Mojica in a swimming pool. The teasing is unrelenting: "Novo the grandiose ivory poet."

To "proper" society, Novo and his friends are monstrous, scandals in full bloom, narcissists incapable of contemplation, parasites threatening nationalist integrity just when Mexico had acquired a new consciousness of itself. Novo and his like are monsters who consider themselves saints, owing to the decline, in the large cities, of physical lynchings. And the unexpected visibility of some gays is taken as a declaration of war, for reasons that are abundantly clear: the invisible is, happily, unintelligible, and that which allows itself to be seen on some level obliges understanding.

To situate the extent of this challenge, we must consult the (very scant) written testimony of his contemporaries. One of them, a poet and physician, recounts a number of episodes to Enrique Aguilar in his very interesting *Elías Nandino, una vida no velada* [Elías Nandino, an Unveiled Life] (Editorial Grijalbo, 1986):[19]

> Whenever we got together or went on an outing, there was always someone who feared Novo's mannerisms, fearing especially that on the street we would be judged on the basis of his gestures, behaviors, or style of dress. But on top of all this, in the normal course of things, Salvador's cynicism was funny, because he knew how to express his ideas with charm; so much so that even those he was offending would laugh.

> One afternoon we arranged to meet at Montenegro's studio, and once there, we decided to go see a play featuring Chela Padilla. We all got into a bus—Pepe and Celestino Gorostiza, Jorge Cuesta, Gilberto Owen, Agustín Lazo, Roberto Rivera, Xavier [Villaurrutia], Salvador, and I don't remember who else. We took up practically half the bus. When we arrived at the corner where we were to get off, Salvador stood up—retouched his makeup, which was very unusual—rang the bell, and shouted: "Here we are, faggots!" No one moved, so then he turned and shouted again: "Heeeeere!" And he pointed to each one of us: "you, you, you . . ." We rapidly got out, like a herd, and once we were on the street, all we could do was laugh.

Novo is exemplary in a number of ways: he is a writer who is always associated with provocation and he is a provocateur who triumphs postmortem because time catches up to his work and attitudes; he is a gay man who lends a supremely talented image to his predilection, and is, without seeking martyrdom, a staunch admirer of Oscar Wilde, without a doubt his model for radical postures; he is a practitioner of the "effeminate," and the emphasis he places on this satisfies the expectations of moral voyeurism; he is a strategist of desire, and, once his youth has passed, extols the power of the purse, which then gets translated into amorous frustration:

> The law of demand and supply
> that taught me the wherefores and why
> delivers love that's easy to buy.
>
> And yet, there are times, when
> the dark veils of hope that died
> are rent with melancholy weeping.

IV

AND PEOPLE NEED TO MIND THEIR OWN BUSINESS . . .

The Homosexual of Mexico—although the term did not exist, nor the intention to incarnate the concept—becomes the mirror of the most reproachable affectation; Novo accepts to a degree the defeat and keeps translating it into an idiom of effrontery, a maneuver that utilizes the infamous in order to mock being famous. For Novo, humor, particularly savage and obscene insolent humor, distances him from the bitterness of reality, and helps him mature psychologically with a rapidity that protects him from "the illusions of the years of youth." From his perspective, to be gay means that one must deny amorous reciprocity, and so his erotic poetry is jocular and semipornographic. In his case, romanticism means not forgiving oneself for anything; it means becoming cynical in order to protect the deepest zones of one's sensibility, and mixing the pleasure of offending others with insults against oneself.

Why not write just to see if perhaps
there comes a sonnet worth more than a dime;
Why not write just to kill time, to cross paths
along the way with an obligatory rhyme.

For I was a writer, and it can't be denied
I was lean as a greyhound bitch;
my jowls have grown fat as my buttocks,
my flesh is fat, my talent bollocks.

What can we do! We must get rich
others should mind their own business
why shouldn't we sell our own hides.

A writer of brilliance, a poet who merits ovation,
from the times of Mister Madero
the very idea is masturbation.

In fourteen lines, Novo dissolves his personal drama with the sharpest irony in a way that implies the abandonment of poetry, the apparent loss of the literary vocation in favor of economic fortune (that impregnable fortress against gossip), the celebration of bought pleasure, the glories of this world made carnivalesque. In this way, satire, enacted against the ideal image of the author, to some degree compensates for "the loss of the kingdom that existed for me." But this is written after a terrible battle, with vast psychological repercussions, against a society that demands hypocrisy and silence.

What would it cost you to say you adore me?
What would it cost me to believe the story,
now we are parted, that you love me?

What would it cost you to kiss me in a letter?
The hours I think of you are indelible
and the charms of my policeman untellable.

The tactic, which is very clear, responds to a culture crowned by *camp,*[20] the technique and cult of gay extravagance that finds aesthetic value and humor in the unexpected, in excess, in the baroque of popular culture, and in the cult of the pose. On the subject of amorous passion, gay self-derision establishes the prudent distance that assuages the vexations of rejection. If anything can quickly cauterize injury, it is cleverness directed against oneself; moreover, by what other means, in such a macho society, can one erase the psychological tattoos produced by terms of disgrace: faggot, whore, deviant, fairy, bitch, *loca* (madwoman), little woman, invert, "Tag! You're it!" In the mechanisms of the ghetto, common to all harassed minorities, vituperation directed at oneself and one's fellows mediates the exterminating thread of macho epithets. "What they are saying to me, I've already said to myself, but with elegance, irony, and a meanness you could never even imagine." In *The Rise and Fall of Gay Culture* (Hyperion, New York, 1997), Daniel Harris describes the process in the United States:

> Homosexuals were drawn to the image of the bitch in part because of her wicked tongue, her ability to achieve through conversation, through her verbal acuity, her snappy comebacks, the control over others that gay men were often unable to achieve in their own lives. The fantasy of the vicious *vagina dentada*, always quick on her feet, always ready to demolish her opponent with a stunning rejoinder, is the fantasy of a powerless minority that asserts itself through language, not physical violence. . . . withering irony . . . became the deadliest weapon of all in the arsenal of the pre-Stonewall homosexual . . .[21]

The construction of the homosexual *from the outside* demands self-hatred, unhappiness as destiny, fatal abandonment of hope. But the project to survive turns inevitably to the self-skinning that—with or without paradox—makes one stronger. Denied the compensations of the circle of Distinguished Couples, disparaged by the anti-intellectual, patriarchal essence of society, Novo mocks himself and, with complementary vigor, mocks the values of those who reject him:

> If I had time, I would write
> my memoirs: volumes of minutiae,
> portraits of enlightened men,
> wise and valiant politicians.
>
> A Proust who lives in Mexico! In these
> pages I would paint the wordless idylls—
> delicious and forbidden—
> of a chauffeur, a robber, a policeman.

It cannot be, so cautious-
ly does my double life define
a single place for every single item.

Let upright men rule my days,
and let me hope in the clamorous night
for the renewing thirst of a policeman.

In his satiric dimension, Novo debunks "good taste" in terms that are all but absolute, perhaps out of his desire to provoke, but more surely because "sordid" expression neutralizes that which expels him from respectable customs. Even if the rhythm of the poetry is subtle, the sudden malevolence frustrates the serenity:

So go. According to the Civil Code,
nothing more is owed; between us, no
accidental family was ever sowed.

Time must help me pardon you.
With thoughts of you—these don't come often—
A certain cleft can't help but soften.

Of those inhabiting the margins, society has exacted a kind of perverse obedience to self-destruction as a norm ("Act as you must, we can't stop that, but don't enjoy it . . ." would be the message); and society expects pathetic behaviors from deviants. As late as 1969, in Mart Crowley's play *The Boys in the Band*, one of the characters declares: "Show me a happy homosexual, and I'll show you a gay corpse." The extraordinary English author E. M. Forster writes *Maurice* in 1913, but only publishes it in 1971, posthumously, thereby imposing [on the work] the conventions of the times, among those the impossibility of a happy ending for moral dissidents. The most that perverts can aspire to, according to the implicit and explicit message, is a tragic sense of oneself, an ennobling of a sorry life with the luxury of sacrifice. Tumultuous death expiates sin, and in a metaphor with meaning for multitudes, the corroded face of Dorian Gray surrenders everlasting youth to a portrait of duty before God and family. The gay man who does not achieve redemptive death is subjected to the trials of individual and collective self-hatred, to which he is condemned by verbal or literary abuse. Here is how Novo describes a friend (Xavier Villaurrutia):

> This little actress, so fine and small
> our very favorite Lilliput
> whose ass accommodates one and all,
> do we exaggerate to call him slut?

In commenting on satire in Mexican literature, Octavio Paz calls Novo a master of the genre. "He had a great deal of talent and a great deal of venom, few ideas and no morality. Weighted with deadly adjectives and light on scruples, he attacked the weak and adulated the powerful: he served no belief or idea, wrote not with blood but with shit. His best epigrams are those that, in a moment of piercing cynicism and lucidity, he wrote against himself. That saves him" (in *México en la obra de Octavio Paz III: Generaciones y semblanzas*). I do not recognize Novo in this portrayal. In his satirical work he does not attack the weak, since, from the time of his conflicts with Diego Rivera, none of the individuals he insults is exactly weak, nor does he adulate those who are powerful. Rather, he laughs at them. (His articles are another thing.) As for not serving ideas or beliefs, the intention of most of his satiric verses, written between the 1920s and 1940s, is to defend against the macho blockade, and survival in a macho country is a very understandable idea and morality. He writes *La Diegada*, the verses against Diego Rivera, after the profane portrait of the Contemporáneos group on a wall of the Ministry of Public Education, and that same logic (responding to harassment with verbal mastery, the only weapon) impels many of his poems. Let me give one example. In *México por dentro y por fuera* [Mexico from Inside and Outside] (Editorial Claridad,

1934), Bolivian journalist Tristán Marof attacks the Contemporáneos in the chapter called "Effeminate Literati":

> In Mexico the traveler or observer is surprised from the first moment by the literary abuse of the word "joto." One would think it some kind of sacred name. The charm quickly evaporates, however, for the literary gentlemen called "jotos" are sad and deviant bureaucrats who work in the lower echelons of government administration [. . .] They have no imagination. Salvador Novo is the author of a book that is boring, pretentious, and intended for certain lesbian women . . .

After this, the response of the one alluded to may be excremental, but it is not an attack on the weak:

To a Marof

So you slithered out of which cunt
in your so-called family,
oozing past chancres, sores, and lesions?
Your sire? The possibilities are legion,
and for your name, it's still an open hunt.

To protect himself, Novo has only his irony, which he uses with full force. If the oppressed are feared, the oppression diminishes. There is an abundance of evidence that for a very long time, life for gays in the ghetto is sordid, with a sordidness born of the isolation of having nothing left to lose, or the terror of being suddenly pulled out of the closet. Paz, perhaps without taking into account the atrocious circumstances of the times, synopsizes the attitude of Novo, Pellicer, and Villaurrutia: "They were honest with themselves and confronted intolerance with integrity and even humor. However, in their writings one does not find the moral independence or intellectual coherence of a Gide or the rebellion of a Cernuda." No, one does not, but rebellion is still palpable in the refusal not to hide, and this in spaces much more asphyxiating than those of Paris in the time of *Corydon* and *If It Die*[22] . . . or even those of Madrid in the 1930s; and there is, in the case of Novo, the insolence with which he distributes "secret" poems and publishes *Dueño mío* and *The Third Faust*, a short play in French. And as for moral independence, that of Pellicer and Villaurrutia is undeniable, as, to a certain point in time, is that of Novo. In a sense, what Bernard Shaw wrote about the author of *De Profundis* after its first publication in 1905 could also be applied to the prebourgeois Novo, the Novo of the defiant pose, of *New Love* [*Nuevo amor*] and the writing of *Pillar of Salt*:

> Our present morality is a repugnant error, and as Wilde could have said, "vulgar." It is not even ethical. Wilde's greatness is based on one fact: our morality could not deceive him, nor could the moralists of his time break or dishonor him.
>
> Until the end, he was true to his pose, because it was an honest pose. For that same reason it was greatly bothersome to him that English morality was also a pose, but without even the pretext of being an honest pose.[23]

THE TRUTH OF HIS TRUE LOVE

Novo's amorous poetry corresponds to that moment in Spanish poetry when the "confessional" tone becomes a strategy for making political that which until then had been disqualified for its "immorality." In Spain's Generation of '27, we see this in the works of Luis Cernuda, Federico García Lorca, Vicente Aleixandre, Emilio Prados. Cernuda writes:

> If a man could say what he loves,
> If a man could raise his love to heaven
> Like a cloud in the light;
> If like walls whose collapse
> Reveals the truth rising from the rubble,

He could make his body crumble, leaving only the truth of his
love,
The truth of his very self,
Which is not glory, fortune, or ambition,
But amorous desire
I would be the one who imagined:
The one who with his tongue, his eyes, and his hands
Proclaims before men a truth unknown
The truth of his true love.
(From "If a man could say")[24]

To proclaim "the truth of one's true love," writers turn to various forms: Villaurrutia in "L.A. Nocturne: The Angels" ["Nocturno de los ángeles"],[25] for example, employs the international gay symbol of the sailor, so present in Cocteau and Genet; Novo opts to enjoy his marginality; and Pellicer affiliates with melancholy clarity:

I know from the svelte and so naked night
that our two bodies were one.
I know from our silence before the darkness
of others, to mute this love that is different.

In *New Love* (1933), Novo's sexual dissidence is expressed in particular details, urgencies, desolations, encoded languages, and even whiffs of the pathetic, false as well as true: confession raised to the level of long-awaited revelation. Highly self-conscious in his work, Novo enumerates the elements of his poetry: "Circumstance, humor, and desolation." To such an accounting, which is essentially correct, should be added a few more items: we must mention malevolence (which offers no forgiveness to the possible innocence of his readers), experimentation, and the analogous execution that avoids a heartrending or expiatory tone.

In *New Love*, Novo's literary character fades out and with it vanity, a taste for paradox, frivolity, and irony as the face that hides the mask. Exhibiting oneself is an excruciating enterprise, softened or disguised by rhetoric in the fullest sense. Confronting his amorous condition, Novo attempts to capture it through a process in which lucidity transcends the iniquity of lived experience: "All we have left is the brief light of consciousness / and to lie down by the side of books." See the definitive poem "Elegy":

> We who have hands that are fit for no one
> repellent to caress, useless for the workroom or the hoe
> long and flaccid like a flower deprived of seed,
> like a snake that delivers its poison,
> having nothing else to offer . . .
> We who have the guilty embittered gaze
> through which the eyes of frustrated Death look out toward
> the world . . .
> We who have rolled through the ages like a rock
> dislodged from Genesis . . .

"Elegy" must be understood in light of the risks and troubles of the homosexual condition, and the accent of *New Love* synthesizes the desperation, the love that is the consciousness of love's impossibility, the transfiguration of disaster: "I entrust to the poem the pain of losing you" or "You, I myself, dry as a broken breeze." The marginal condition is a failure already inscribed, the epic of that which has failed to happen, the never-ending sadness of happy days that were never lived.

The least important question is whether this corresponds, or not, to biographical reality. Novo complies with one of the demands of the period: given that amorous relationships between "abnormals" are inadmissible, he who carries out literary treatment of sexual or moral marginality requires the poetic landscapes of solitude and bitterness. In making manifest his wretched spirit, Novo expresses in the poems that which he represses socially: his emotionality and his eroticism. In this he is not alone. Even Pellicer, in a strange moment in his poetry, speaks as one who has been expelled from any paradise:

> For those who have spent their life watching for What Others Say
> and who without looking at the rags of their own solitude have
> been gladdened when others have been glad;
> for those who have wept with the innocence of the desert sun
> that does not know it illuminates the skeletons of caravans;
> for those who have screamed from the highest peaks of midnight
> in a solitude so solitary it's unbearable to see,
> I gather my voice as though it were the last thirsty sip of my life
> to tell them of the horrible beauty that fate has sent me.

Pellicer plumbs the depths of a desolation without limit:

> I do not know what crimes course through my blood and pervert
> my fate, why my destiny holds such depths of desperation . . .

A precursor of this confessional poetry, the Colombian Porfirio Barba Jacob (1881–1941), who also used the names Miguel Ángel Osorio, Main Ximénez, and Ricardo Arenales, and who long resided in Mexico, to some degree also coincides with Novo and Pellicer. Always excessive, a venal journalist, a poet of ardent lyrics, Barba Jacob considers himself the perfect *outsider,*[26] so implacably opposed to any positive image of himself that he does not hesitate in going to the extremes of political abjection, of sordidness, of ostentatiously displaying the most condemned "vice" of his time (marijuana). Barba Jacob considers himself essentially a *poeta maldito*, or "damned poet": "My plan is to shock the bourgeoisie . . . I spread my happy word, my delight in joking, my homosexuality, my doubts, my drunkenness." Everything in order to support the dark legend that, in isolating him, provides the protection due an eccentric and grants the exaltation of his marginality, and is all the more painful for being moral rather than economic:

> Those of you who have not borne in your heart the burial
> mound of a god
> nor on your hands the blood of a murder;

Those of you who do not comprehend the horror of
consciousness before the Universe;
who do not feel the worm of cowardice
constantly gnawing at the roots of your being,
who merit neither ultimate horror
nor ultimate shame . . .
Those of you who have not shuddered in horror and fear,
as though between two hard bars, in the iron embrace
of an evil passion,
while the soul burns with raging brilliance,
mute, morbid,
vessel of opprobrium and lamp of universal sacrifice,
You cannot comprehend the painful meaning
of this word: A MAN!
(From "A Man")

"OH BODY, FOR SHAME."

At forty, defeated by the rules of the deterministic game, Novo considers himself old, and there are numerous proofs of this:

—Were you thinking you would write?
—Well, if every
night I could write a sonnet . . .

—Say that Destiny
is your handicap. That gelded and bootless
you turn in vain to look back.

That the mirror proves you are done for;
shows skin that was once caressed,
sagging around a body that is grotesque.
That everything is over. That the dreamed-
of happiness . . . That in a moment you hadn't dared hope for,
you hope for . . .
—Then I am well and truly reamed.

In 1951, in the play *The Young Man II* [*El joven II*], the youth is surprised by the wretched maturity into which he has entered: "How you disgust me! With your flabby muscles, drowning in fat, with your bald head sunk in pillows, full of dead numbers and dead words."

The reason for the despair: he is no longer an object of desire. According to the beliefs then in vogue, the loss of one's attractiveness marks the beginning of one's posthumous trajectory. Like Baudelaire, the gays of the time could have exclaimed: "Oh Lord, give me the strength and courage to contemplate my body without chagrin!" Thus Novo, in *New Love*, written when he was twenty-nine, fulfills himself erotically with the nostalgia that flows into the mythologizing of all he once had. If the most relevant aspect of the *other* love[27] ("the evidence of the crime," Novo would say) is its always chimerical character, these poems describe the abyss of one who sees the end of his corporeal eligibility. Without the advantages of marriage and descendants, the poetic personage accepts the compensation (the aesthetic of isolation), and the loss of that ultimate consolation: self-deception:

> I must drown it in these tears.
> Eyes without hope see plainly:
> that life bears lovely fruit,
> then turn to the mirror
> only to see that the smile lies,
> the body is gauche and ungainly.

Heterosexuals of Novo's generation do not have these problems. How could they confront them, when the patriarchy denies women the right to exercise their taste, their faculties for rejecting "[bodies] that [are] gauche and ungainly"? Novo, like every gay man of those years, accepts the Faustian bargain: you will have a few years for your hallucinatory immersion in promiscuity, and then you will deliver your soul to sudden old age, with all the uncertain prospects inherent in the deal. The trade-off seems unjust, but what else is there?

V

PILLAR OF SALT

I emphasize the obvious: the challenge of *Pillar of Salt* must be located in its own moment, not from a boastful postmodernity informed by Stonewall, ACT-UP, and Queer Studies; or by Genet, Derek Jarman, Keith Haring, Robert Mapplethorpe, and Reinaldo Arenas, among many others; or by *Savage Nights*, *Philadelphia*, and the jubilant ending of *In and Out*, the film by Frank Oz. In 1945, to write (with the obvious intention of eventual publication) a memoir of different lust[28] is an act of enormous bravery. Novo knows, with an abundance of detail, that he is the object of scorn and mockery, and for this reason I believe that he settles in to his triumphalist version of homosexual mobility and fixedness, of the compensations and castigations that overtake those who interrupt their ascent and turn, arrogantly, to watch the punishment of the cities of the plain. For reasons very worthy of consideration (to stir up scorn is to incur multiple risks), it is clear that public confession, before a wide horizon of known and unknown readers, assumes among other things the risk of absolute psychic nakedness. The project of the book is abandoned, and in doing so, Novo very possibly renounced his most vivid and personal prose.

At the beginning, *Pillar of Salt* is the account of an extraordinarily precocious child in Mexico City, who remembers Justo Sierra (Minister of Education), and a little houseboy with whom he has "that first and perhaps definitive experience." The child's upbringing is, one might say, chaste. In Jiménez, Chihuahua, where the family moves, he is schooled at home, and the professor decides to caress him:

> . . . and he placed his hand on my fly. With great delicacy, he asked, What do you call this? Anus, I told him, because that was the name my mother had taught me for penis. Since he didn't seem to agree with that alteration in anatomical nomenclature,

> that night I tried to verify it with my mother, referring to my tutor's lesson. It is quite possible that this discrepancy provoked his dismissal.

The account, a small gem of comic literature, equivalent perhaps to the description in *Return Ticket* of a spinster's attempted seduction of Novo, is, like everything in *Pillar of Salt*, in the service of sexual obsession. Already in Torreón, in the days of the Revolution, Novo witnesses the assault of the *villistas* [Pancho Villa's troops], which culminates in the murder of his uncle Francisco; he watches the courtship of the servant Epifania; he studies in a school for girls; he organizes transvestite play in the attic of his friend Napoleón, who proudly announces to Novo's mother: "Salvador and I are the two effeminates of Torreón"; . . . and he accepts the initiatory rite. In a brief little play, Novo has the role of the rich boy:

> . . . [even with] the applause, the full auditorium—the only thing that made me vibrate, and the only thing that has remained indelibly engraved in my memory, is the furtive instant when Jorge called me into the dressing room where he was making himself up to look like an old man for his recitation of his "Recollections of a Veteran," and taking my head between his two hands, pressed his moist lips against my own.
>
> That secret, which was at the same time a revelation vaguely expected, filled me with an intimate happiness. It was the triumph of my beauty, the realization of my wish to have a boyfriend like the girls at the Model School, the possibility of penetrating the mystery of the empty room to which the unknown man had carried Epifania. I waited, heart pounding, for the next step this boy would take—this boy whose presence I inexplicably hadn't noticed all year, and whose dark slanting eyes, smooth white skin, and red mouth now owned my sweet secret. While he seemed older to me, he could not logically have been more than three or four years past my own twelve.

Novo's double fascination becomes transparent: the evocation of himself, with his ability to recapture experiences of delight, and the presentiment of horror on the part of his readers, who merely by casting an eye on his pages become his accomplices. They learn how a pubescent homosexual is initiated in Torreón, Mexico, and, in return, cannot then claim innocence on the subject:

> The morning we finished our exams, the school emptied out. . . . When [Jorge] verified that no one was there, he appeared in the doorway and called my name. It was everything I'd hoped for. With great caution, trembling with emotion, I went to him.
>
> Without saying a word, he pulled me to him, squeezed me hard, and pressed his mouth to mine in a long, wet kiss, his tongue penetrating all my senses, its sweetness flowing through my entire body leaving me with an acrid taste of tobacco. Without letting go of me, he lifted his hand to his fly and extracted an erect, reddened penis that he tried to put in my hands. Horrified, I pushed it away. I had never seen anything like it, so enormous, so veined. Seizing my mouth again with his, Jorge wrapped his hand around his penis, from which I saw spurt some thick gray drops that hit the floor. Only then did he let me go and, with the rag used to clean the blackboards, carefully wiped from the floor what he had wrung from his enormous worm.

The bildungsroman, the novel that charts the progress from youth to maturity, finds its form in this case through the extraordinary nerve of an essentially autobiographical writer who takes pleasure in showing that which he considers normal because it is inevitable, but which others will judge highly pornographic.

After the basically mechanical sexual initiation, the move to Mexico City, and the discovery, while studying at the San Ildefonso high school, of the city, of literature, and of cinema:

> The nobility, strength, and courage of the heroes worked in me, germinating an adoration of their mythology, and little by little, I discovered with astonishment that I was in love with one of those heroes. . . . I was humiliated, not by the thought of being *abnormal*; not by the fact of feeling for this man a desire and a passion that I was incapable of condemning, of considering as culpable; but rather by the fact that my feeling was without a doubt so singular, made me so unique, so strange in the world, that if my hero were to know of it, he would probably feel nothing but contempt for me, would humiliate me, hit me instead of kissing me.

In the selection of memories, the determinative criterion is what will scandalize the confessor or psychoanalyst in every reader. Thus, the flamboyance of his makeup, (". . . to apply . . . all the creams and all the powders in her overflowing cabinets, and to polish my nails with her beautiful ivory implements, and to arrive at school full of vanity . . ."); thus, the imitations of Italian divas; thus, the warning "that my sin was less singular than I had believed"; thus, his acquaintance with the eccentric beings of the *sidelong world*.

WHERE EVERYONE ENDS UP IN THE SAME PLACE, BECAUSE INCLINATIONS ARE A GEOGRAPHIC BOUNDARY

In *Pillar of Salt*, a basic theme is the entry into the homosexual ghetto, *entry into the milieu*. As in no other of Novo's texts, this is the subject that gives him the impetus and opportunity to display his great descriptive talent, which, in a few lines, gives literary density to his notable or archetypal characters. With Novo, and thanks to the system of "sexual concessions" among the characters, the ghetto imparts its secrets, its manias for preciosity, its acuity for nicknames (the cruel tag that time makes indelible), its infinite network of factions and friendships, its internal solidarity devastated by the logic of a minority without pride that believes itself to be the cause rather than the object of persecution. The gay ghetto of the 1920s: that "incredible, dispersed, nocturnal, embarrassing, and brazen realm," populated by those marked by the sensation of only being recognized by their appetites, the constant surround of mockery and self-mockery. According to histories of sexuality, there are rules in these circles, and the same ones are found in very different countries; among them: fleeing the norm means giving up happiness and an amorous life; "bitching" (the exchange of mutual insults) is the incessant reminder of the measure of scorn from those outside [the ghetto]; "verbal transvestism" is obligatory because the closest identity for the "weirdos" is feminine, and the result of contagion; relationships among gays do not work (". . . for in his judgment, one *sullied oneself* by sleeping with those of one's own sex"); an exclusive relationship is clearly inferior to promiscuity.

There is no such thing as the sudden appearance of the gay universe in Mexico City. It was already all there—in the catacombs known by those who knew and that existed with rigorous nocturnal discipline; the perpetual lying in wait for conquests; the frustrations and groaning stories of forced exiles and family scenes that exploded in words to the effect of "Get out!"; with beings living a double life, acting happy and audacious in the ghetto but dull and starched at their jobs. What *Pillar of Salt* exhibits is the rhythm of social dreams: for heterosexual heaven to exist, it requires the detailed construction of homosexual hell, a hell consisting of searches, scorn, and social harassment:

> Having discovered the sidelong world of those who understood one another with a look, I was finding those looks just by walking down the street: Avenida Madero, where, in the evenings, people went for a leisurely stroll. There, always guarding the door to El Globo, with his cane, his gaiters, his silk jacket, his gaze behind his pince-nez casual but alert, his waxed gray mustaches, was Señor Aristi, called The Ass that Squeezes; through the connecting door to El Globo one went up to the office of

> *licenciado*[29] Solórzano—who, according to Ricardo, sang opera arias (*Ninon, Ninon, que fait-tu de la vie*), and who was called Tamales because he made his conquests by inviting youths to an early supper of "a few little tamales and a beer." Along this strip would come Mother Meza, on the hunt for human goods and clients, who never slept with the merchandise he procured for his buyers, the refined survivors of Don Porfirio Díaz's regime.

The image of the whole is one of enormous desolation. A world ruled by the hunt and by commerce, by hope, self-loathing, and the jeering derision of one's fellows is one that adjusts itself—whether or not it wants to—to the most negative versions of heterosexual life. However, at the same time it encourages a sense of humor and imaginative flight. Novo lacks explicit solidarity with the human landscape he describes, but his bravery is the highest form of solidarity that was possible at the time. Sarcasm, satire, lyric desolation, ingenuity, and social brilliance are forms or methods to give voice to those who at the time are considered unworthy of using language.

The profound friendships: Xavier Villaurrutia, Delfino Ramírez. The entry into the literary world. The conquest of the city and the deployment of his powers of seduction. If there is one unavoidable conclusion: a life lived with passion, and that hurts no one, justifies itself; and *Pillar of Salt*, irresistible to read, is Salvador Novo's message to Salvador Novo: if what you lived was inevitable and enjoyable, you have no cause for regret. Novo writes to be read one day, and to be read, in the moment of writing, by himself. For this reason, *Pillar of Salt* is no mere provocation; first and foremost it is the exercise of rights denied. And for this reason, what was once "unspeakable vulgarity" reappears as a brave testimony to the change in customs and to the exceptional being who, with no explicit program, accelerated social changes and created a magnificent literature wherein our diversity is enriched.

Pillar of Salt

SALVADOR NOVO

MY EARLIEST CHILDHOOD MEMORIES appear as fragments, disjointed, with no continuity. Tardy and injurious attempts at psychoanalysis have salvaged from among them recollections of my most primitive stages of libidinal development, others that were lodged with especial strength in my memory, and some my doctor helped me recognize as particularly significant. Having spent my life in the company of a mother barely fifteen years my elder, my normal development stunted by an oedipal complex I am too cowardly to fully confront, I have made occasional anxious efforts to reconstruct with greater clarity the circumstances of my birth and youngest years. And so I learned that my father, a Galician, was thirty when he married the cheerful, robust, provincial brunette of fourteen or fifteen who was my mother, the youngest of four daughters in a family of nine children in Zacatecas. The head of that household blithely went through the family's money, and when he died at the beginning of the last century, he left my grandmother, who had an admirable talent for getting along, the problem of raising and educating their numerous brood.

The eldest of the four sisters, Virginia, married a North American who lost no time in leaving Zacatecas and establishing himself in Mexico City, where their four children were born: Lilly, Edna, Fred, and Ruth, who is exactly my age. My mother likes to recall that, at the time, she herself was closer to her brothers than to her sisters, was tomboyish and quarrelsome, intuitive and clever in school. When my father, after having lived in Havana, settled in Zacatecas and fell in love with her, the clever girl saw a swift marriage not so much as the culmination of real affection on her part, but rather as her opportunity to escape the confining life she had at home. The wedding took place quickly, as soon as my mother's family, whose older boys had started working for the railroad, moved to Mexico City, where the infatuated Spaniard followed. My parents took their honeymoon in Aguascalientes; but they returned to the capital for my birth, which occurred on July 30, 1904.

I have also learned that I was alarmingly late in learning to pronounce the letter *r*. As for other childhood traits, I have heard myself described as indiscreet (I would tell certain visitors what my family whispered about them, or reveal the nicknames we had for them among ourselves), and prone to fix, with my own hand, anything I considered to be flawed. It is also said that when they took me visiting, I would run to inspect the bedsheets, and often pronounce them ugly or soiled; and once, my aunt Maria surprised me in the living room of her house, where I was painting mustaches and stripes on the portraits in the family album. When she cried out, I looked up and, with all tranquillity, pointed to the portraits on the walls and explained, "I still have to finish all those."

Maybe it is natural in children, but in my case I think it necessary to emphasize that my father's image disappears almost entirely from my childhood memories. I know he was slender, blond, with light-colored eyes, but I can barely remember any of his interests or activities. Later I have a much clearer recollection of his making things with his hands. I remember, as though it were a dream, that he made a plaster lamp for the bedroom that gave off a soft light. His modus vivendi, his versatility, which later I also observed with greater precision, led him in my youngest years to try his fortune by opening a butcher shop, for whose inauguration, replete with fireworks and a party, we made paper chains of pink and china blue; or by taking part of the house and turning it into a tailor's studio—no doubt to spring himself from his meat slicer's job in a grocery store downtown.

My mother's image, on the other hand, has always been clear, full, and vigorous. I would go out with her in the early evening to visit my grandmother, or a couple with two children my age, or simply to take a walk, stopping on our way to buy treats for dinner. I would go out with her in the morning, after she returned freshly coiffed from her beauty shop, and take a horse-drawn carriage to the consulting rooms of Dr. Porfirio Parra, who tended me for illnesses I no longer remember.

It was always my mother who came for me at the Herbert Spencer *kindergarten*. Of that establishment I only remember two things:

once they made us plant orange seeds and on another occasion they selected me to sing at an important school festival to be held at the Teatro Arbeu, with Don Justo Sierra, a government minister, in attendance. Sowing the orange seed in the garden of the *kindergarten* greatly intrigued me. For years afterward, I dreamed of returning to the spot and gazing at the tree that had been born, miraculously, from that seed. As for the festival, I remember clearly that the song they had me sing demanded I be dressed as a Neapolitan organ-grinder, with blue velvet shorts, a cap, and the instrument strapped to my chest; upon taking the stage, I was to gesture leftward to the wings, and sing:

> I come from those mountains
> beyond the sea.

That is all I remember, other than the melody of those lines, which suddenly rises up from the reservoir of my five- or six-year-old memory, which has also conserved the blurry image of Minister Sierra in the act of giving out diplomas, and how some photographers made me climb up onto the lid of a sky-lit toilet in the Teatro Arbeu to pose me for pictures that came out in *El Mundo Ilustrado*—in whose archives the photograph must still exist.

On that occasion, as on practically every other day, my mother dressed me with fanatical attention. She adored the curls she combed around my forehead; she powdered my face; she made me purse my lips so my mouth would stay small; and, with the same inhibiting objective, she made me always wear shoes that pinched my natural development. A photograph from that time, which I still have, immediately brings to life the tortured recollection of the day I was taken to the studio, on foot, wearing shoes that hurt me horrendously.

My uncles loved me in the same admiring way. Proud of my beauty, they would take me out strolling with them on Sundays. My uncle Paulino, the eldest, would pick me up and buy me sweets and balloons in the Alameda. I also remember that one of those Sunday outings must have coincided with the opening of the Amphitheater in Juárez, because the crowds got in the way of our usual walk.

This is the period of my first sexual memories; though discontinuous and disjointed, they are recounted here in close proximity. We had at home a little servant, named Samuel, with whom I used to play. When I played alone, making altars with my blocks and empty cookie boxes, I didn't need anything or anyone else. But when I played with that boy, I wanted us to pretend to be mother and son, and he then would have to suck on my right breast with his hard lips and erect tongue. This caress filled me with a strange pleasure, which I only recaptured many years later, when in a moment of exquisite surrender, I recalled that first and perhaps definitive experience, which may have been the original trauma that explains the formation of my adult libidinal predilections.

In the house next door lived some North American kids, one of whom, somewhat older than I, was occasionally my playmate. I don't remember if we always did this, but one time we hid under his dining room table, covered by the tablecloth, and he, opening his fly, invited me to touch what he called his plantain. And so I did, until his mother, who lay ill in the next room, shouted out to us. They spoke in English, which I didn't understand; but a strange intuition made me understand that the boy was defending himself to his mother against the accusation of a sister who had come in on us unexpectedly. What had happened, he explained, was that he'd been telling me how the previous Sunday they had gone to Vallejo—this word I remember with total clarity—and bought plantains.

The boy's sister must have been as sexually precocious and aggressive as he was, because another time, at my house, she came into the bathroom, lifted her skirt, and made me lick her sex. I remember the taste, which was salty, and her clitoris, which looked like a tiny nipple. Another curious heterosexual experience occurred with my cousin R. My uncle Manuel had just been awarded his medical degree, and my cousin and I would play doctor and nurse in his office, which he had set up in my grandmother's house.

R. was the nurse, and I had to give her an enema, but with my penis in the "normal" opening, which she presented to me naked. I shied away from the operation, explaining that we should try her anus instead (and here I lied through my teeth), because at school they had told me that the other way, worms would come out. The experiment was never in any way consummated, needless to say, neither in the manner she seemed to want, nor in that which I said I preferred.

I showed signs of having a good memory, and my mother, who read a lot of poetry, made me learn "recitations" even before I entered elementary school. I knew "Guns and Dolls," which I declaimed with studied gestures, and delighted in the whole anthology from which it came. The "Cantor del Hogar"[1] was then a prominent figure. They said his poems had been translated into many languages, and were much admired for the references to his unfortunate private life, the details of which I managed to overhear. And so, on the day of his funeral, when his sumptuous cortège proceeded down Calle Guerrero, we all leaned out of the window to watch it go by, and at home we talked a great deal about that poet.

I don't why, but upon entering the official elementary school near where we lived, instead of starting in the first grade like everyone else, I was immediately placed in the third, with boys who, naturally, were older. I suppose the entrance exam indicated that I knew more than was usual, and thus justified that they advance me according, let's say, to my mental age. My sudden immersion in that dirty classroom, with those impoverished boys, was extremely unpleasant. The smell and touch of a certain green ink—*alizarina*, I think it was called—found in the inkwells of every desk, is associated in my memory with anguished afternoons spent practicing my clumsy penmanship, and with the recollection of an incident that was destined to seed, or nourish, my guilty inferiority complex. It happened that one of the boys, maybe even my *gringuito* of a next-door neighbor, gave me a mildly pornographic sepia print of a naked woman. An older boy, who caught me looking at it between the pages of a book, seized the print and threatened to denounce me to the professor unless, every afternoon, I brought him all the sweets he wanted. Alarmed and submissive, I accepted the blackmail and for many days complied with his conditions. After our midday meal, I would ask my father for money and, on the way to school, I would buy those sweets, which I saw as my own inexorable complicity in the secret of my first moral transgressions.

Two fragmentary memories allow me to date to 1911—when I was seven years old—the period when my father left for the northern region of the republic, where we soon joined him, to seek our fortune, or obliged by circumstances, or impelled by a spirit of adventure that I certainly did not inherit. There is the memory of the furor that marked Madero's[2] entry into Mexico City, a nightmare midnight when I awoke in my parents' arms as the doors rattled, and people threw themselves into the streets beseeching the heavens; and there is the impression of having read, as an enormous headline in an Extra edition of the *Imparcial,* the words PEACE, PEACE, PEACE, referring to the end of the revolutionary rebellions in the north. Very soon afterward, my mother and I would board the train for Chihuahua, to join my father, whose brothers were storekeepers there.

The one who lived in the city of Chihuahua, the one my father had gone to join, was named José; he was older than my father, less blond, and had a large mustache. They had to have been together in Zacatecas, because Uncle José had not forgotten his unrequited love for María, my mother's older sister. Even I, who adored her, called her "My sister María." At the train station in Mexico City, as she kissed me one last time, María offered to send the supplements to the Sunday papers to cheer me up; and they always arrived promptly, with her letters, at the grocery store run by my father and Uncle José, in whose back rooms, my mother and I, torn away from her family, were slow to adapt to that rather provisional, pioneering life. The difficulties clearly challenged and inspired my father to keep struggling, even without my mother's cooperation, which in any case he couldn't have hoped for, since she plainly didn't love him and had no interest in helping him forge ahead to build their family fortune. My mother's attitude was one of hard, silent reproach for a man from whom she had expected that, in payment for their notorious difference in age, he would have showered her with comfort and riches, without her giving more than her unresigned tolerance. In the face of my father's delicate health—doubtless owing to which I am an only child—my mother dug in to life in her early twenties with a sullen strength, with a will to survive made evident by her vigor. Uprooted from the affection of her mother and siblings, far from turning her attention to my father, she invested it fully, tumultuously in me.

For my part, I, too, found in her caresses a refuge against our displacement and separation from my loving aunts and uncles in Mexico City, which from then on was imbued with the symbolism of an objective; we were in exile, unjustly and provisionally, on a peripatetic adventure in a hostile world to which my mother and I declined to adapt and which we could not accept as our place of residence. From Uncle José's store we moved to downtown Chihuahua, and I began studying at the school annexed to the Institute, of which I remember only isolated visual details and my friendship with the Valderrama boys—Salvador, Ángel, and Sergio. In the mornings, the cold was horrible. In *Return Ticket*, I believe I sketched the fragment of an impression of that winter, when water froze in the faucets and, one day, on the way to school I saw a dead dog crystallized on the sidewalk.

My memories now are clearer or will become so in Jiménez, Chihuahua. My father had evidently secured a good position with the Casa Russek, a large store, and soon we were settled in that little village. The house we lived in was enormous. It gave onto three streets. Two or three large rooms separated by a wide hallway faced one street; forming a right angle with other rooms, they also looked out on another street. Yet another angle was formed by the big dining room, which connected to a different passageway leading to the kitchen and continuing out to the yard, whose gates opened to the street that ran parallel to the one in the front of the house. All of the bedrooms gave onto the central patio, which had a little well near the dining room, and a rustic little garden that flourished without tending in that agreeable and fecund climate. My father installed a swing for me in the center of that garden; and when I wasn't playing with the yard animals—the lambs, the hogs, and the hens for which my mother began to show some condescending affection as our placid life fattened her up—I enjoyed long hours on that swing. But this last move upset my discipline at school. In Chihuahua I had repeated the third grade, but I'm sure I didn't finish it, given that they registered me for the same grade in the Jiménez public school. I'm not very clear about the order of my educational experiences during that time; which is to say, I don't know if I was in the official school before I studied in the little private one across the street from our house, or after; nor do I have a chronological sense of those two schools with respect to the teacher who came to tutor me every afternoon at home, closing the doors to the dining room where we had my lessons, and who may have enhanced my progress at other schools or weakened it, I don't know, owing to my inhibitions surrounding these memories. It's possible that, owing to the Revolution, then at its peak, the official schools were frequently closed, and private ones were temporarily taking children in. In any case, my recollections are clear with respect to each of these three separate pedagogical experiences. The little private school was the cottage industry of two unmarried sisters, the Señoritas Rentería, one of whom would eventually become one of Pancho Villa's widows. There they mostly taught me religion and drawing. I found it soothing to draw, again and again, a cross adorned with forget-me-nots. As for the teacher who came to our house, he had me read while he watched. One afternoon, he decided to caress me, and he placed his hand on my fly. With great delicacy, he asked, What do you call this? Anus, I told him, because that was the name my mother had taught me for penis. Since he didn't seem to agree with that alteration in anatomical nomenclature, that night I tried to verify it with my mother, referring to my tutor's lesson. It is quite possible that this discrepancy provoked his dismissal.

The official school was a disagreeable reproduction of the one in Mexico City. Populated by poor kids, many of whom had no shoes, its director was a solemn and squalid teacher who suffered from a bad complexion. Only a few of the boys were sons of families with whom my parents had begun to form friendships in the village: the Galvaldóns, the three Botello boys, two older than me and one my own age, all very pretty, the youngest of whom was my friend in class and my playmate at home. Although at school I abstained from mingling with the others, I could not escape their whisperings. That is how I learned that the beautiful Botellos had been the sexual victims of someone somewhere who had lured them into a car—*cochado*[3] was the verb they used. From that very instant, I developed an interest in cultivating the friendship with the boy who was in my group. An investigative interest, much colored by the need to affirm and assure the validity of my own narcissism. As a game or a joke, or out of instinct, the boys went around kissing the Botellos, as they laughingly referred to them. But they stayed away from me. Not because I didn't want the caresses of any of those boys, all of whom I found ugly. What I needed was proof of my own beauty, more objective than the simple adoration I was accustomed to at home; an assurance that the public attention, the admiration, expressed in the caresses of those boys at school, would have offered. But the assurance didn't present itself; and from then on, I was impelled toward exhibitionism and a compensating mythomania. So I would bring that Botello boy home, and after running around for a while, I would make him sit with me on the swing, where I would draw out his statistical secrets. How many times had they kissed him that day at school? I don't know if we weren't both lying when we each confessed to two or three times. Then we would kiss, and perhaps, truly, it was the only kiss, out of so many we boasted of, that either of us had been happy to receive.

The domestic staff at home was composed of a huge family of a mother, two or three daughters, and a typical invert of a son, whom they openly called "Juan the faggot." With his straw hat always on his head, he happily carried out the feminine household tasks, helped his mother in the kitchen, did the washing, ran errands, fetched me at school. But I kept him at a distance, I don't know if owing to my parents' vigilance, or to my own repugnance and hostility, but I constantly made him the victim of mean tricks. I remember once I caught a fly, called him into the dining room, and when I had him within reach, opened my fist, and shoved the fly into his mouth, rubbing it against his teeth, as triumphant as I was irritated by his docile resignation to my constant cruelties.

Still, it was he who, in a casual way, sowed within me an entirely new spirit of sexual investigation. We received a visit from a lovely girl named Epifania, who had come from Chihuahua, where she had been one of our servants, only to disappear one day without any explanation. Now dressed very elegantly, she talked at length, crying a little, with my mother. What had happened to her? Why didn't she want to come back and be our servant? Juan the faggot confided, with an air of mystery, that she couldn't return "because what had happened, happened"; and I couldn't shake another thing out of him, except that she had run away with a soldier. So now she was a lost woman, and her fate was to develop syphilis, the name for which I don't know how I first learned, but which seemed to me the natural consequence of physical contact, the realization of which I didn't yet understand. What, concretely, "had happened to" Epifania? I tormented myself imagining a scene whose composition I was totally at a loss to fill in. I drew an empty room, without a single piece of furniture, in which I forced myself to place the familiar figure of Epifania; but—the man who had carried her off?—And as for "what had happened to her," what could this consist of?

The girl returned one afternoon while my mother was out, and I resolved to question her directly. But all I managed to do was make her laugh as I persecuted her, wracked as I was by a curiosity as intense as it was frustrated, so that the frozen image I had within me of that empty room, without a single piece of furniture, was gradually dispossessed of the familiar figure of Epifania to be replaced by me, awaiting the consummation of that mystery in which the unknown person was a man capable of robbing someone, which he did in the secret of that empty room.

I liked that little village very much. I enjoyed its afternoon rains, which left the trees on the road to the railway cleansed and green, and which formed pools where frogs would start to grow that in a few nights would be croaking interminably.

When I returned from school, or accompanied a servant girl to market, and I was carrying the basket, I used to approach those pools and catch tadpoles, which they called *tepocates*, and which I tried to grow at home; or at least I'd watch them every day of their development, from when they had a tail until they started losing it and began happily leaping everywhere. Other afternoons, the mystery of creation offered its rapture in the flowers that opened only for brief, precisely defined instants in the sad garden outside Russek's store, where my father worked; these marvels were in memory much greater than when I saw them again, disappointed, many years later. Closed and withered in the morning, at five in the afternoon their corollas opened in the form of stars.

Without a doubt, our family was important in the village, and that circumstance satisfied me. Our house was one of the largest. So rambling, in fact, for the three of us who inhabited it, that it wasn't even all furnished, nor did we visit all of the ample rooms except at night, when my father, holding a light, made the tour of them, making sure that all the doors and windows were tightly shut. On Sundays, my father took me with him to the barber, and then we'd sit while he chatted with his friends and I drank lemonade, in one of those casinos, hotels, or large arcades the Spaniards established in all the villages of the republic, and in which innocent provincial Sunday leisure was full of cigar smoke and the sound of dominoes, until it was time to go home and eat; and then after, if there were bulls, we would go together, and then return for my mother and head for the theater, when there was a play, or we would join the improvised promenade on the dusty road that led to the station. My father liked to show me off, dressed as I was as a sailor, crowned with the curls that my mother dressed, and which had to have seemed not only an anachronism but a Porfirian challenge from this family "from Mexico City" to the appearance that was more normal for kids from a north at once already a little Yankified and revolutionary, to put it simply. A photograph we kept shows me, proudly dressed as a sailor, in the act—stage-managed by my father—of pointing with my finger to a star, while he, seated and attentive to my nautical explanations, looks at me with interest and satisfaction.

With respect to my future, what could it be? My parents, especially my mother, continued to believe that our provincial life was only temporary. Her goal was to return to Mexico City, be reintegrated into her family; and its justification was the natural fact that I had to be a doctor, like my uncle Manuel, and could only study to be one in Mexico City. When I thought about it from that perspective, I accepted it without argument, and even enthusiastically looked forward to a return to the multiple affections of my uncles, and I would go about gathering from the garden the plants, leaves, and roots with which, through magical infusions, I would surely create marvelous medicines. But, on the other hand, the theater we used to see was awakening in me the vague desire to become an actor; but in the depths of my soul, what I wanted was to stay just as I was, cosseted and pretty, taken up with the little intimate pleasures of accompanying the servant girls to market in order to carry the basket, of playing with the boys at home, of drawing my crosses and forget-me-nots, of propelling myself so furiously on the swing that I ended up almost horizontal at the level of the roof; sheltered in that enormous house, where swallows nested in the hallway beams and flew back and forth to the puddles full of placid frogs.

But doubtless I was unaware of circumstances that would end up moving us from Jiménez, if not yet to Mexico City, which was the settled goal of the family plans as they pertained to me, but to [the town of] Torreón. Those circumstances were born of the insecurity caused by the constant upheavals of the Revolution, which endangered small villages. Torreón offered my father better opportunities for work than a store detested by the revolutionaries, which they would eventually burn down, and better protection for us all. In addition, one of my mother's uncles had been living in Torreón for some years, a brother of my grandmother, about whom I had only heard the family in Mexico City speak, with utmost respect, saying that he was an imposing, almost legendary figure, whose characteristics I managed to puzzle out only a good deal later, after a brief but direct acquaintance that came of living with him, then learning of his tragic end, and probing into later revelations, which a process of induction also helped clarify.

He was tall, corpulent, and bald, with big bulging eyes. He lived absolutely alone. Upon the death of his mother, my great-grandmother, whom he adored, the good son had shown himself to be an excellent brother to my prolifically fertile grandmother, whom he helped in many ways so she could move to Mexico City, while he tried his luck in the north, and made a fortune—dented by his taste for gambling—in a host of transactions that involved buying and selling seeds and cotton. In a more recent time, he devoted himself to building houses, which at first he would live in and then sell; then he would build another one next to that one, giving it the same fate. He began these operations on Avenida Hidalgo, almost directly opposite the famous Chinese laundry, where Villa had had so many people assassinated. The first house he built there was very different in style from the next, which he kept and rented out. The next one, also very large, was almost at the corner of Calle Ramón Corona. That one he sold to some Greeks who ran a business at home making seltzer; the last adjoining house he built was his own residence. Farther on, the block ended with some humble cane shacks, near the road that led into the dry mountains.

This house had the singular trait of having its structure arranged in a cross formed by its corridors, thus creating through this configuration four independent bodies of rooms, two of which gave onto the street, each with a separate entrance. Beyond the main entrance, a tiny garden preceded two adjoining rooms, which shared a bath, and which faced the corridor opposite the block of rooms with direct access to the street that were occupied by Uncle

Francisco as his library and bedroom. Then there was the patio that formed the arms of the cross, with the kitchen and toilets to the right, and to the left, two large dark rooms, one of which was the dining room.

It is obvious that all these details of a house, my indelible memories of which extend to minimal details of color and decoration in each one of its parts, just as they used to appear in my frequent dreams; and just as they accompanied my anguished desire to return to visit, to know if it even still existed—I couldn't capture all of these sights the first time we came from Jiménez to visit Uncle Francisco. On that occasion, he lifted me in his arms and, kissing me, carried me to his bookshelves, which I gazed at with admiration; he took down from those shelves a few of the little onyx figurines to give me, and invited me to choose a book to take with me, and through nothing more than chance, I selected a certain *Voyage on the Nile*, which seemed to please him very much. Somehow it was determined that we should move to Torreón, and that we would live in this house that belonged to Uncle Francisco until we found one of our own. That's how urgent the reasons—as yet inaccessible to me—must have been for our move.

After having shared his voluntary solitude, we left Uncle Francisco's house to occupy one that was vast and far away, on the road toward the Alameda, which was then lonely and depopulated. It was out of the question for me to go to school, any school. All of them were closed because of a revolution, because of disturbances, battles, constant shooting, which so distressed my parents that we shut ourselves up inside and watched the passing hordes of *villistas,*[4] or whatever they were. Houses were searched at whatever hour, and any photograph, document, or newspaper was used as proof against anyone considered suspicious, and resulted in that person's death, and the pillaging and burning of his house. We happened to have in the house a lithograph of Madero, and my father's political astuteness was evident in the dangerous guess that if the bandits ended up in control of the population, and proceeded to search everyone's house, the picture would come to our rescue as they gazed at the redeeming sign of our complicity—the effigy of the Apostle placed in a highly visible spot in the living room; what they wouldn't know, from this minute inspection, was that the usual unseemly refuge of the safe-conduct lithograph was behind the plank that served as a seat in the latrine of the far patio. This is exactly the kind of revolutionary farce that "La Adelita"[5] tried to ennoble, by way of inspiring ill-defined hordes of pillagers. One very famous female brigand came to our house and asked for water, but she made all of us drink from the same glass before she did. What a wise and rustic version of Catherine de' Médicis.

All these circumstances indicated it would be best for us to return to live with Uncle Francisco. He himself came to our house to convince my parents that it was absurd for us to keep living in that isolated and distant house, when we would all be safer in his sufficiently spacious house. The situation was increasingly anguished and unpredictable. The *villistas* were about to descend on the city. He exhorted us to move in with him.

I wrote about this incident, with the unmitigated feeling that infused its first evocation, in *Return Ticket*, when, in spite of my constant tendency toward autobiography, I didn't think I would need to relive that anguish. I don't know if even now I could improve on the picture of that nightmare that is, despite the pretenses of the Revolution-addicted members of my generation, the true image, the true impression of those who, at a young age, experienced from up close all the senseless brutality of the Revolution.

The moving truck had just finished unloading our furniture at Uncle Francisco's, at about two in the afternoon, and my uncle and father seemed nervous. The *villistas* had just entered the city with their usual shrieking, shots fired in the air, and horses galloping through the streets, now deserted but for them. The activity of the move must have attracted the attention of a group of outlaws on horseback, who with great din and racket called at the door. Before our door was opened, my uncle Francisco and my father moved a long ladder against the wall of the house my uncle rented on Avenida Hidalgo, and which at the time was unoccupied. It was my mother who opened the door, outside of which had gathered many curious onlookers who lived in the neighboring shanties. The bandits said they were looking for a certain federalist, and as they explained this to my mother, Uncle Francisco opened the door of his apartment that gave onto the street. As soon as they saw him, the bandit chief yelled, "There he is!" and fired his pistol. Uncle Francisco managed to close the door, run inside, and reach the ladder with my father. It didn't occur to those men that the door opened by my mother was part of the same house, and while they set about demolishing the one closed by Uncle Francisco, a humble woman living near the first house he had built on Avenida Hidalgo, and who knew him, tried to save him, saying that he was not the one they were searching for; that the federalist lived around the corner and that she could lead the way.

Those bandits believed her, and they followed her. But the timing[6] of the events had been determined by Destiny. Once they reached the corner, Uncle Francisco and my father had ended up escaping from the house on Avenida Hidalgo and started running down it. As soon as the bandits saw them, they didn't hold back. Mixed in with their shouts and shrieking, my mother and I heard two shots, and then we saw them streak back to us, break down the door, burst in, and begin the pillaging in which all the greedy inhabitants of the adjacent shacks took part.

I have never seen my mother more pale, or more serene, than at that moment. She took me by the hand and led me next door to the house owned by the Greeks, whom we barely even knew, and placing in their hands a small bundle of money and papers, asked them to take care of me, because she was going to go back to the house, where they would probably kill her. If that happened, if she didn't come back for me, and my father, as she supposed, were also dead, she begged them to communicate immediately with Mexico City, and to send me to her family's address, which she was leaving with them.

I stayed there for many hours, while my mother witnessed the sacking of our house, and suffered the kicks and insults of those outlaws. Finally that night, it was confirmed that my father was alive, and that only Uncle Francisco had been assassinated. But my father, a Spaniard, had to stay hidden, for the hatred that Villa had for the *gachupines*[7] was well known. So my mother did even more. She went to see Villa. That Hottentot told her that he already knew that the boys had made a mistake in killing her uncle. For that there was no remedy; but what he could do was pardon her *gachupín* husband. This he would do, provided he leave the country the very next day, and for which he gave her a safe-conduct with his disgusting signature, which we kept for a long time as a monstrous curiosity.

My father went to El Paso, Texas, and my mother and I stayed in that desolate house with its long, interminable nights of the terrifying moon, of tragic silence. The first days, while they were in the process of returning our house, we were taken in by the Díaz de León family; but after that we lived alone, attended by an old cook who didn't sleep at our house, and were visited only by the Greek neighbors whose friendship we began in that way to cultivate. They were two partners named Gianacopoulos and Kypurós. While the former, who was tall and bald, went out in his little mule-drawn cart to distribute their seltzer waters, Pane Kypurós stayed home to manufacture them, which left him time to pursue many other hobbies, such as building a piano key by key. His Mexican wife was named Margarita, and she had already given him two sons, Take and Basilio, both considerably younger than I, but still I played with them. Soon a third, Jorge, was born, on the occasion of whose baptism those good and honest neighbors strengthened their friendship with my parents by inviting them to be godparents.

I suppose that Villa's hordes ended up leaving the city to extend their controlling claws over the entire north, for my father was finally able to return from his exile. He brought us many gifts, and had refined his original plans to go into business in Torreón, for which purpose he had acquired in El Paso merchandise that he thought he could sell easily and lucratively. Once more, we were going to set up house where, even more than before, I would be the center of everything. Doubtless I had grown in those months, more than my father had imagined, so that among the gifts he brought was an adorable pair of sandals into whose coquettish shape I could not manage to insert my already considerable foot. On the other hand, I greatly enjoyed a gray sweater, which in the mirror endowed me with a feminine silhouette accentuated by my movements, for this was the moment in which I was to leave behind my childish clothes, a period when the sportswear worn by the young today did not exist, and one went abruptly, without any transition, from sailor's suits to the graceless, austere clothes worn by adults, with only the difference of short pants and the fibrous stockings made from *popotillo*,[8] which I detested.

I liked then to transform myself, to dress like a girl or woman. I played theater games at home with the Greek boys, and at night I insisted on going with the servant girls on their errands, so as to mix in with the "scruffy ones" who gathered to listen to the songs and *corridos* sung by a blind man who scratched at his guitar by way of accompaniment. It enchanted me to undertake these excursions in the early dark, wearing my mother's shoes, as though to challenge people to discover how I was shod, or invite them to find fault. On one of those evenings, I was standing as part of a group listening to the blind man, when I felt something warm wetting my leg. I understood immediately what had happened: one of the "scruffy ones" was urinating on me. But instead of moving away, or denouncing him, or protesting, I let him do it, seized violently with sudden, indescribable, unfamiliar feelings of voluptuousness.

It seemed a foregone conclusion that I would not pass the third grade in public school. I was trailing behind, since I'd never been able to be present for a whole term, and I was much too young in Mexico City to take that grade; in Torreón, the only private school, the Model School for Girls, admitted a few boys, me among them, and so again I resumed my third-grade studies as imparted by the cold, languid Señorita Inesita. The school emphasized religion and sacred history, which I knew very well; most afternoons were dedicated to embroidery, sewing, and other such disciplines from which they tried to isolate me by giving me short stories to read or lessons in history, while the girls took up their embroidery hoops and, with their needles and silken thread, plucked out strawberries and leaves for napkins, the most expert among them embellishing cushions with English lace. But I couldn't concentrate on my reading. I found it odd that they didn't assign me embroidery tasks, which I was certain I could accomplish, and I asked the girls to let me help them. A few were beginning to talk of sweethearts. They shared their secrets, conspired to position themselves next to the window so as to see those fellows pass by, and, vaguely, I imagined a boy who would come down that street in order to see me embroidering, who would smile, giving me a sign of his love. What was happening all over again, but more clearly now than at the school in Jiménez where I identified with the Botello boys, was that now I was imitating the girls of the Model School. The contradictions in the rules that restricted the boys to a small patio during recess, separated from the girls, whereas in class we were all together, underscored in my eyes the injustice of a sexual discrimination that was as irritating as it was incomprehensible.

Of the four or five boys who represented the stronger sex at that school for girls, Napo, whose affinities were notorious, quickly became my most intimate friend. He was restless, mischievous. The only son of a mother separated from his father owing to the latter's growing business interests, he and she lived alternately with his maternal grandparents and with his uncles, in one of the very large houses in which I used to stay to eat at an enormous table presided over by the grandfather, an immaculate, austere, distinguished old man who resembled the portrait of a gentleman from days gone by, whose French goatee and gray mustaches inspired silence. The ceremonious meal concluded, Napo and I would shut ourselves away in the attic, which was full of his mother's hats and dresses, and with which we organized an orgy of disguises.

But in spite of these feminine weaknesses of Napo, which united me with him, he nonetheless had within him, undoubtedly due to those *ranchero* origins that gave his family vast holdings in cotton-producing properties, a virile aptitude for other games that I completely lacked. It was customary then for the boys to go swimming in the "cuts," or dirty streams, that flowed from the Nazas River when it was high; it would never have occurred to me to do this if Napo hadn't dragged me along. When he saw that I didn't know how to swim, he took me to another one of his houses, an enormous place near the Alameda, which had a pool, and where he showed himself to be the best of teachers. I wanted to imitate him, and nearly drowned. My mother forbade me from trying again to swim.

To Napo's innocent, spontaneous indiscretions, which spilled without malice into my mother's sensitive and alert mind, I owe two kinds of repression, which doubtless in some way determined my later development. Once, while his mother was visiting mine, Napo entered the living room that had been converted from Uncle Francisco's library, and without any reason whatsoever announced in a loud voice that "Salvador and I are the two effeminates of Torreón." Accustomed to his *ex abruptos*, his mother simply told him that we should go out and play. Mine kept silent; but from that day on, she let me know that Napo no longer charmed her. Very soon afterward, upon returning home from school, I found my father artificially enraged, ready to whip me with the rope he was holding in his fist. He gave me a few lashes, and in the midst of a sob born more of surprise than of pain, I learned that my mother, who was watching the scene at once impassive and satisfied, had informed him that Napo had told her that I was planning to run away and join the Children's Theater Company—then headed by one Armando Arreola who still works there in that profession—which performed at the Carpa Pathé, where my father used to take me on Sunday afternoons; while I admired the company, no such confidence had passed from me to Napo, nor had I even defined for myself such an adventure. Doubtless in this way my mother displaced onto Napo half the guilt, represented by my desire to escape, which is to say, my heterodoxy; and she restored to my father an authority rarely invoked, at least with respect to me, her own exclusive possession; his symbolic act of punishment, her irritation and desire for revenge for a revelation about my character expressed crudely by Napo in her presence, assumed the character of an intolerable publication of the secret, which had been until then a form of cohesion between my mother and me against my father, and against the world.

At the end of that year, Napo's family sent him to El Paso to study agriculture, which would be useful for their business interests. He wrote me from there; but my mother opened the letters, and in answer to one that seemed particularly confidential, she dictated to me the one in which I broke off our friendship forever.

While communications with Mexico City were being reestablished, and my grandmother and uncles were coming to Torreón to deal with Uncle Francisco's will, the house from which he had escaped into death was rented to a large family with whose kids I played when I returned from school. I completely forget the name of their boy who first inspired that tender, pure, silent desire for his presence that years later I tried to reconstruct in the poem called "Love," in my book *Mirror*.[9] I could not now improve on that image. He never knew what it meant to me to sit by his side after watching him play athletic games, to feel with the rise and fall of his tired breath the coming of the night that would separate us.

That same fruition, that same intimate voluptuousness without a precise object, by whose warmth I felt anointed every time I found myself next to that boy—all of whose physical features have been erased completely from my memory—I would feel again, at other times, when I left the house after eating and entered the cane shack where our old cook lived. The eldest of her children, Trini, was a bootblack, and in the afternoon, like everyone else in Torreón's stifling summer heat, he would take a siesta, stretched out on the floor of his stripped-down room. I would stealthily open the door, enter, and kneel down to contemplate him, empty of all thought, of any intention except to engrave in my own senses the image of his bare feet, his dark chest, his sweaty neck, and his peacefully sleeping face. I breathed in, as one more mystery, the spicy, acrid smell of his flesh.

My libido, however, was still very far from reaching what might be called an objectively genital stage. One time, while my parents were leaning against a window, I heard in the street the familiar braying of a rutting donkey, and I drew closer in order to see, just at the moment when one animal was mounting the other. My parents quickly closed the window and led me away. They must certainly have overestimated my perspicacity, just as they did on the night they gave me careful instructions for politely turning my back, when the surprise arrival of a young Spanish señora from Chihuahua made it necessary for her to sleep with me in my bed. I never managed to understand why they insisted that I keep a distance from her, when at no time did I feel even the slightest curiosity that might have encouraged me to do otherwise; and she, for her part, must have considered it bizarrely premature to encourage fascination with her sex in a child who was so sleepy, so inept, and so tender.

Without friends since Napo's departure; with only the occasional company of my taciturn father, who incessantly smoked long black cigarettes, and who, during the time we lived in the city, taught me to play chess, I had to drown my tedious solitude in reading. Uncle Francisco's books were many and heterogeneous. I read them in their self-same disorder. From this facile immersion: a knowledge of and exclusive disposition my parents didn't share; in these books my narcissism soon found a new wellspring. My capacity for imitation manifested itself in obvious parodies of the facile academic verses I was reading, and of the very nineteenth-century prose in those volumes. I sucked up Narciso Campillo's *Rhetoric* and applied all of his simple prescriptions.[10] Suddenly I found myself writing sonnets, satirical verse compositions, and odes "In the manner of," whose handwritten originals I still have in a notebook that I titled—inwardly certain that literary glory awaited me and that I mustn't deprive posterity of a single crumb of my talent—*My First Poems*, dated 1915, that is, when I was eleven years old. Not one of those poems shows genius; but there is not one that doesn't exhibit real talent, above all a talent for self-exhibition: a mimetic, even histrionic agility, and decorous representation of styles lacking in sincerity and authenticity.

Satisfied that I didn't go out to mix with the bad company of the local boys, my mother made no opposition to my separating myself from life with long hours of tranquil reading. That was how she kept me close, and it seemed she was happy enough, though not terribly interested, that I was writing poems. But this habit, too, would soon receive the traumatic intervention of her authoritarian vigilance. I had read the first volume of *The Man Who Laughs,*[11] and in Uncle Francisco's pillaged library, the sequel was missing. I asked my father to buy me the complete work, and he, who in the face of my literary affinities showed an incipient, anxious pride, hastened to do so. But the edition he found, in that store where he always bought my toys, and where he had bought "the magic lantern" that I still have, was an illustrated edition (published by Maucci), one of whose plates showed the naked heroine struggling with the monster. And my mother, who believed it her duty to leaf through the book, convened a quick family council with my father, the point of which was to proclaim it necessary to supervise my readings, and, of course, to proscribe *The Man Who Laughs*.

That prohibition, which imparted to my readings a sinful character, lent them a never-before-experienced enchantment. From then on, I read with a vaguely investigative industry, as one who has just discovered that there exists a secret, and is resolved to find it.

As soon as our communications with Mexico City got reestablished, our life again was oriented toward the capital, which stirred up memories and projects for the future. The first emanation from Mexico City arrived with a pathetic letter from my grandmother, whose reading out loud unleashed in my mother a crisis with much weeping, liberating her from many months of stoic repression. "Not a leaf in a single tree moves but for the will of God," my grandmother wrote, as though to conjure and communicate to my mother a dolorous resignation to the fact of her beloved brother's death. In that letter, my grandmother announced that before she herself would come, two of my uncles, Salvador and Guillermo, were to arrive imminently to begin the investigation of assets left by Uncle Francisco, about whose business affairs and fortune none of us knew anything, and of which my grandmother would be the natural heir.

Of those two uncles, Uncle Salvador treated me like a child, and Guillermo like a slightly younger brother. They both intervened in the matter of my clothing and hairstyle, which they found anachronistic; above all, they talked to my mother about my education. But Guillermo took a particular interest in the fact that I wrote verse. It seemed to him completely natural, because he, too, wrote poems, and recited them for me. We examined Uncle Francisco's books together, we compared our readings, and as he was leaving, he offered to send me books from Mexico City that in his judgment would help me perfect my poetry writing.

Soon after, my grandmother arrived, accompanied by my Uncle Manuel, a doctor, and Julia, the youngest of the unmarried daughters. While my grandmother, pale, terse, and fine, established her natural majesty in the house, and directed with admirable aplomb the clarification of Uncle Francisco's tangled affairs, which immediately revealed that a usurer was in possession of documents that would leave in his hands almost all that Francisco had left, my uncle Manuel reverted in Torreón to his city vices of languor, sleeping late, taking obsessive care of his person—all of which, to his hedonistic cast of mind, were rights conferred by having a university degree. So it was Aunt Julia who granted me the most attention and cultivated my admiration for her capital-city elegance, shown off in large hats, in boots with infinite buttons, in outfits that were light-colored and cheerful. Extraordinarily slender, sickly since childhood, she had always been favored by my grandmother, who spoiled and cosseted her. They brought her to the theater, and she knew the latest songs and dance steps, which she taught me. She appeared to be exultantly happy, and during the days she spent with us, wrote frequent letters to the sweetheart whom she was soon to marry.

Their return to Mexico City filled the house with anticipation. We were to follow them as soon as I completed my primary studies; then I would enter Preparatoria, and become a doctor like Uncle Manuel. This would happen in only one year, as I'd already completed the third and fourth years at the Model School for Girls, and was taking the fifth in Professor Verástegui's very small private school strictly for boys. The Valderramas, whom we knew in Chihuahua, went to this school, which at night was converted into a commercial academy offering English, accounting, and shorthand, and which my father wanted me to attend. My mother objected. There was no point to it, given that I was going into medicine, not business. The most she would accept was to have a professor from this school come in the afternoons to give me private lessons in English. I hated him. He was very big, full of energy, and had an amputated leg. He would set his crutches next to the chair where he sat and made me repeat lessons from that Robertson Method, which began, *Peter and Fanny, a True Story: Peter was a handsome boy, with rosy cheeks and a turned-up nose*. I was absolutely certain that I understood nothing, that I would learn nothing of that language, nothing that came from the teaching of that monster who didn't spoil me, who usurped my afternoons.

The disagreeable image of that professor is associated, merged, with my memories of the last school I attended in Torreón, where I completed my sixth year and therefore my whole primary education, which resulted in the inevitable return to Mexico City. As a counterbalance to, and refuge from, the hard reality of both, I practiced a superstitious religion, at once magical and commercial. When I didn't want the teacher to ask me questions in class, all I had to do was to say prayers. I had already made my First Communion, in the small church of El Carmen, with a Spanish priest who had imposed penances as light as my sins must have been; and from the practice of that ceremony that so easily liquidated my sins, I had derived this mechanism for trafficking, trading prayers for favors, to be granted in advance or retrospectively, and this is as far as my religious fervor went.

The new school was enormous. The classrooms assigned to the first years bordered two patios, which during recess boiled over with boys of all ages. The room for the sixth grade was situated between those patios, and looked out on the street; it was presided over by an aged but robust professor who, from the moment I arrived, took a dim view of me, and assigned me the desk farthest away from his reach, next to a tall, skinny boy who dressed always in jackets with white piqué, and whose bony, yellowish hands scribbled down notes on everything the professor dictated, as he passed among our desks, exercising his right to swat at the heads of boys gazing elsewhere, as though he were batting at flies.

In vain, I tried to win his favor. I read well, answered his questions. He soon discovered that numbers would never be my forte, and so he passed me over for the presentation of every other assignment in order to humiliate me at the blackboard with arithmetic, and so justify his desire to punish me, which one time brought him to the extreme of shaking me, hard, by my hair. Even though I had suffered this agonizing situation in silence, making no other protest than my silent prayers, that time I couldn't help but cry when I got home, and had to confess to my parents that the professor had hit me. My father went to discuss the matter with the school director, a picturesque, pockmarked fellow with greasy hair. I don't know what they talked about. But from that day on, the professor no longer addressed me, and plotted against me with the boys in my group, ordering them to boycott me absolutely. "Men don't whine or tell tales," he used to say to the others, on whatever occasion, so that I would understand the reason for my isolation.

The end of the school year: for the boys and for the school, it meant that those who had been classmates for several years would from now on be dispersed; but for me, the imminence of our reintegration into Mexico City lessened the artificial tension of our relations, and even though it failed to soften the professor's attitude toward me, the fact that he would soon have me out of his sight forever seemed to induce him to treat me with greater tolerance. Before the examination period, he granted us a few days to study and prepare; during that time we also had to rehearse the literary-musical program and install the exhibition of manual arts projects that would officially close the year. One day they got us together, and in front of the director, tested our voices to see who recited best. Against the professor's will, I was chosen for the central role in a small theatrical piece, in which I would play a spoiled little rich boy, a liar who receives his just punishment: an ingenuous version of the moral tale about the boy who cried "Wolf!" And when there really was a wolf, his friends were so accustomed to his false alarms, that no one came to his aid.

During the recitation auditions we were subjected to, the professor ardently recommended Jorge González. In truth he had a full, clear voice, with beautiful timbre, and he declaimed with elegance and grace. It was immediately decided that he should learn "Recollections of a Veteran," by Juan de Dios Peza, and perform it at the closing festivities.

The rehearsals, in this brief vacation before exams, allowed me to leave the house in the afternoons and, for the first time that year, cultivate the friendship of my classmates, some of whom were in the play. After rehearsal, there was time to head for a field where some other boys were playing baseball, and my fellow actors would join them. I merely watched. I threw myself down on the warm ground, under the setting sun, in the beginning of winter, and savored this new sweetness of calm and simple friendship with those kind boys. I remember three of them: the one they called "Negrito" Villarreal; another slender redhead who was poorly dressed, whose name I've forgotten; and Alejandro Patiño, dark, with curly hair and large dark eyes, who played piano. The first two would already be working in the coming year; "Negrito," who was an orphan, would assist in his uncles' store. Alejandro would continue his studies in Saltillo.

During rehearsals, when I was waiting my turn with Jorge González, I noticed, little by little, that he kept his eyes on me. The development of our complicity escapes my exact recollection. Perhaps it began with a shock, as sudden and yet as mature as the opening of a rose that had been for so long a bud. Even with all the nervousness, the importance of this opportunity to let my histrionic abilities shine on the night of the festivities, and all the events that surrounded the culminating ceremonies—the applause, the full auditorium—the only thing that made me vibrate, and the only thing that has remained indelibly engraved in my memory, is the furtive instant when Jorge called me into the dressing room where he was making himself up to look like an old man for his recitation of his "Recollections of a Veteran," and taking my head between his two hands, he pressed his moist lips against my own.

That secret, which was at the same time a revelation vaguely hoped for, filled me with an intimate happiness. It was the triumph of my beauty, the realization of my wish to have a sweetheart like the girls at the Model School, the possibility of penetrating the mystery of the empty room to which the unknown man had carried Epifania. I waited, heart pounding, for the next step this boy would take—this boy whose presence I inexplicably hadn't noticed all year, and whose dark slanting eyes, smooth white skin, and red mouth owned my sweet secret. While he seemed older to me, he could not logically have been more than three or four years past my own twelve. But he wore long pants, and smoked, and played baseball on a school team the existence of which I had only just discovered.

In the following days, he searched me out, with a naturalness that amazed as well as pained me. Only after walking a little toward school or toward home, I would be haunted by a vague wish that I wanted him to make concrete; I was anxious to hear the magic word, the wished-for formula with which he would reveal the whole mystery of his desire and how, exactly, it might be realized. What is it he wanted us to do? Why didn't he tell me clearly? "You know," he kept repeating, "you know what I want."

The morning we finished our exams, the school emptied out. Only three or four of us had stayed in order to stand guard in the rooms with the exhibitions of manual arts projects. Jorge was in charge of the room next to the one I was watching. When he verified that no one was there, he appeared in the doorway and called my name. It was everything I'd hoped for. With great caution, trembling with emotion, I went to him.

Without saying a word, he pulled me to him, squeezed me hard, and pressed his mouth to mine in a long, wet kiss that tasted acridly of tobacco, his tongue penetrating all my senses, its sweetness flowing through my entire body. Without letting go of me, he lifted his hand to his fly and extracted an erect, reddened penis that he tried to put in my hands. Horrified, I pushed it away. I had never seen anything so enormous, so veined. Seizing my mouth again with his, Jorge wrapped his hand around his penis, from which I saw spurt some thick gray drops that hit the floor. Only then did he let me go and, with the rag used to clean the blackboards, carefully wipe from the floor what he had wrung from his enormous worm.

I ran from the room, confused, fascinated, disconcerted, torn between the infinite pleasure of that long, unforgettable kiss, and the anguish of that disgusting ejaculation. When I reached the door, I stopped. A man was watching me, as though he had been waiting for me to come out, with cold, green, cynical eyes, as though he already knew what had happened inside. I froze, looking at him, not knowing what to do. Then he smiled, came forward, took me by the arm, and walked with me to the school door, all the while explaining that he already knew where I lived, and telling me that he would come to see me that same night, so we could chat; he would whistle like this—he showed me how—and said that I was to tell my parents that I was going out to play, and then I should meet him on the corner.

We were finishing supper when that expected whistle made my heart beat faster. I told my parents that I was going to play for a while with the Kypurós boys at their house, and went out into the street. Intense moonlight bathed the silent night. Leaning against a door, that man was waiting for me, so we started to walk, I guilty and with my head down, he insinuating and victorious. He began by confiding that he knew what had happened between Jorge and me. He was the school's baseball instructor, and knew all the boys well, none of whom kept secrets from him. As he spoke, he looked at me lecherously, licking his lips and holding me tightly by the arm. I beat a retreat. I swore to him that nothing had happened between Jorge and me. What could happen, if we were both men? And truly, that was a question I formulated as a negative, a hope behind the disguise of an impossibility.

To this he made no response. He was pleased, not because I found it impossible *to do anything* with any man, but because *I would not have done it* with Jorge González, because Jorge González wasn't deserving. He was a very perverted boy. Just ask the trolley conductors. I wasn't to bestow my affection on him—or offer him anything else. The man telling me all this, who must have been about twenty, proposed that he himself topple my idol, and take his place. Hearing him speak ill of Jorge certainly threatened, dissipated, disoriented my affection for him, in the sense that he shattered the illusion that I was the only person Jorge loved; but it did nothing to draw me toward the informer, on the contrary, I retreated further, repeating the elusive statement that I *would not do anything* with a man. He then slowed our pace to stop before a dark door, and vaunting his athletic vigor, asked, "Not even with me?" fixing me with his green, jocular stare, and smiling, only to smother my indecisive "no" with the cold contact of his lips.

But it was already very late. From our hiding place, we glimpsed my father, who had gone to look for me at the Kypurós house and, disconcerted not to find me there, was heading home. I freed myself from the arms of that man, promising to see him the following night, and ran home to lie about the reason for my being out late, and to enjoy in my bed, the minute recollection of an entire day full of overwhelming emotions.

At the risk of breaking the structure, the continuity granted by my selective or intentional memory of these childhood recollections, I must mention, here on the threshold of the consummation of an experience with that baseball player that would establish forever the form of my sexual satisfaction, two circumstances, each of which left its mark on my developing libido. The first was my discovery, in books, of the image of the feminine genital apparatus. Among Uncle Francisco's volumes, the one I was most taken with was called *The Physiology of Marriage*, by Amancio Peratoner. But it was not so much my reading that captivated me as my absorbed contemplation of the images, which were drawn in minute detail and showed the characteristics of virginity and stages of deflowering; these pictures revealed to my astonished eyes the mystery of the other sex, fleshy and open to receive that which on my body was beginning to be covered with a soft down, and became erect before the provocation of those images. Through this visual stimulation, I achieved an anxious tumescence, satisfying in itself, which did not impel me to discover either masturbation or the spasm of detumescence; I was afraid, however, of being surprised as I was looking at those drawings, of having my enjoyment found out. My first ejaculation occurred not in the usual forms of auto-eroticism, but in circumstances of peculiar anguish, with neither erection nor tumescence, but happened one day when I wanted to take a trolley home, and couldn't, however fast I ran, catch up with it. A combination of anxiety, of hurry, of near desperation took hold of me, injecting a strange tension in my muscles that pressed on my testicles, and released a wet electric charge that had nothing to do with the sexual feelings I had had while looking at the plates in *The Physiology of Marriage*.

The second circumstance that could correctly have channeled my sexual development was my closeness with a blond girl who had just arrived to be our new house servant. Until then, and despite my being able to attend to the details of my personal hygiene, there was still a female servant assigned to my care, a kind of anachronistic nanny. She dressed me, went to fetch me at school. She used to reproach my laziness, and I would retort that when I was grown up, I would hire the services of those who would do everything for me, even chew my food. But that servant, already a mature woman, had never incited my sexual curiosity. The new girl, however, seemed to me to have been chosen to prove with her own flesh the location and form of the organ revealed by the plates in the secret book.

When we were alone, or close, I tried to touch her, and she did not resist. Finally, one night when my parents went to sit outside in the doorway, as families did then to take the air, I found the girl in the bathroom, lifted her petticoats, and clumsily approached her with my erect penis. I didn't, however, manage even to touch her. At just that moment, we heard the signature sound of my parents dragging their chairs in for supper, and she went running to the kitchen, leaving me with a frustration for which she could not be held guilty; but if not for that, and for the involuntary but inopportune and definitive interruption of my parents, the experience would have been not less, but much more, definitive and traumatic.

A few days passed between the episode of my culpable nocturnal escapade and the afternoon on which the baseball player would satisfy my curiosity. If Jorge had known how to reach me; if, as doubtless he wished to, he had arranged a place where we could hide ourselves away, my first contact would have been anointed with passion. But Jorge no longer sought me out, and so with the other boys who in the end had become my friends, I went every afternoon into the countryside to watch the team play baseball, and after a game that he had coached, and in which he was a *fielder,*[12] Pedro Alvarado, as I now knew he was called, came up to me and we returned together to the city, almost reaching my house. We talked about how I would soon be going to Mexico City, and how we wouldn't ever see each other again. He suggested I give him something to remember me by; and guessing what that would be, I agreed to call for him at his house the next afternoon.

He lived near the school, in a humble little house. When he saw me arrive, he got up from the bed where he'd been stretched out and put on his jacket; we walked almost to the entrance of the Hotel Washington, where the Lerdo and Gómez Palacios trams used to stop. From his pocket he took a few pieces of flannel of the kind used for baseball uniforms, and handing them to me, he told me to wait for the Lerdo tram to come and go, and then to pretend to have just gotten off, before going into the hotel and asking for him. I was to say I had fabric samples to show him for the team uniforms. That is what I did. An old woman, visibly habituated to such diaphanous strategies, looked at me scornfully and led me, by way of a creaking staircase, up to the second floor, to the very door of a room that he opened to admit me, already in shirtsleeves, as though I'd interrupted his siesta. Within there was a large bed with its headboard against the wall. Pedro closed the door, locked it, then, embracing me, led me to the bed. Under his pressure, I turned my back, closed my eyes, and let him do what he would; with an expert hand, he undid my trousers, touched and handled me with consummate skill, so that I felt not the slightest pain—nor even a minimal pleasure—upon feeling myself penetrated in an act that I imagined equivalent to the deflowering described in my book; in reality, what I felt in my flesh was similar to the slight discomfort I felt during the introduction of the enemas I was subjected to at home when I was sick. And I neither saw, nor touched, his penis.

1917. Watching the landscape through the train car window as we returned to Mexico City, I recollected, with singular introspection, the five long, pregnant years since I'd been seven until now, when I was leaving behind everything that had endowed the agonies, revelations, and discoveries of those years with all their intimate enchantment. My health had not been perfect. Treated with Quina Laroche tonics and cod liver oil, I almost died twice, first from a powerful intestinal infection, later from malaria. Both times I was attended to by Dr. Viesca Lobatón, one of whose daughters was my classmate at the Model School; the first time he saved me from the stupid treatment of an expensive doctor who wasn't even embarrassed to be called Diamante ["Diamond"] Mihaloglou; the second time I almost succumbed to fits of burning shivers brought on by eating too many of the black figs one Sunday when my father took me to those magnificent nurseries cultivated by the Chinese in Lerdo and Gómez Palacio [near Torreón], where they also produced the delicious grapes, melons, figs, and peaches served from large colorful trays at our celebrations of my saint's day, which fell during the most fruitful time of the year. After these illnesses—and perhaps because they coincided with "growth spurts"—I remained thin and weak, needing a hygienic and sun-filled life, which my mother preferred to replace with restoratives and reclusion. Soon enough, I also had problems with my teeth, and suffered horrible treatments from the dentist. I think our first trip from Jiménez to Torreón was to have a cavity filled in a molar—and it was done so consummately well that it's still good. But that was not the only operation I was made to suffer. Doctor Viesca Lobatón, who was truly concerned for my health, discovered that I had nasal polyps, and he removed something resembling a grain of white corn. He also said that when I had developed a bit more, he would extract the adenoidal growths in my larynx.

In my sickly condition, I was more like my father than my mother, who barely remembered arriving in Mexico City with one foot in her coffin, owing to an acute peritonitis, from which Dr. Parra saved her without an operation; and never once since then, neither in the north nor in Mexico City, did she ever again get sick; she kept her admirably white, even, strong teeth, her abundant black hair that she would brush defiantly in the face of my baldness, her smooth dark skin without the slightest wrinkle, her good sight, which she stubbornly refused to assist with spectacles, and eyes she squinted myopically, out of sheer coquettishness.

My father, on the other hand, was always pale, slender. He would sit quietly for long hours holding a long, black, smoking cigarette between his fingers, which, like his blond mustache, were stained by nicotine; there was a faraway gaze in his eyes that were such a light shade of green they were almost yellow, like his hair, which was curly and fine. Only now do I understand and admire the strength of his will and the determination of a struggle he was ill-suited to sustain in the face of my mother's predominance over a passively submissive household, in an environment that must have been alienating, vaunting as it did the audacity of northern males. A flagrant inferiority complex, originating in his impotence (or rather its direct cause), had established in my father the mechanism of abdicating to my mother's authority, which allowed him to protest in silence, in apparent conformity, as he silently developed new schemes for economic prosperity that would eventually restore his strength and authority. My mother let him be, as certain as she was desirous of his next failure, removing him more and more from any intervention in a world in which I was already taking his place. When my father's habitual cough, the sound of which announced his tired return home, became drier and more frequent, when he began to live in a permanent haze of fever, with a strange, glassy brilliance in his eyes—which he attributed to a cold he caught at the Turkish bath—my mother coldly diagnosed him as consumptive, quarantined him in a solitary bed, and forbade him the pleasure of kissing me or even touching the toys and books he bought me whenever he could.

I made common cause with my mother. Proximity to my father, to his tired breathing, the odor of his clothing and black cigarettes, began to disgust me. Our return to Mexico City had offered me the image of my uncles—well dressed, perfumed, happy, and obliged to praise and spoil me; the stooped, defeated, weak, sad figure of my father didn't fit with this picture. It was out of place, an obstruction, an unwelcome addition. Old Laius in the way as Oedipus comes down the road.

Would it be anything other than a late and useless gesture to his memory to consider how my life might have developed if, in the fight for me, my father had won, and if I, from a young age, had helped him in his various businesses? Nothing is lost in dreaming that, if instead of pinning the family hopes on our return to Mexico City and my earning a university degree, I could have learned the practice of commerce, shared work and worries with my father, gotten involved in the same activities as my classmates at the Escuela del Centenario. The office he opened for his timid mercantile operations, over whose door hung a small sign: Andrés Novo, Merchant & Commission Agent, could in time have expanded to become Andrés Novo & Son, and after the founder would have caressed his grandchildren and peacefully closed his large green eyes, become the office or store of Salvador Novo.

But I could also have accepted the offer of a scholarship to study at the Ateneo Fuente de Saltillo and become a teacher. With all the ill will my sixth-grade teacher had toward me, he couldn't manage to have me disqualified from the government scholarships for the students who scored highest on their exams. But my mother wouldn't even consider a possibility she considered ridiculous. With the completion of my primary education, her exile had now ended. Now I had to begin Preparatoria, and she, who had left without fully measuring the consequences, had returned, the prodigal daughter, with a son all her own, for whose destiny she alone would be responsible.

In the five years since she'd left, my mother's family had only experienced the change of separation from its eldest son. My uncle Paulino, the model son for his numerous little orphan siblings, had assumed the overwhelming task of supporting the family with a position at the railroad (when the real eldest son, Roberto, was determined not to be right in the head, he was radically amputated from the household by my energetic grandmother and from then on lived apart). Paulino had already seen his good works crowned with the rise in the medical profession of his brother Manuel—the "Collegiate One," as my Aunt Virginia called him—whose specialty in venereal diseases guaranteed a good income; and by the docility with which his brother Salvador followed him into an honored position with the railroad, and by the fact that the youngest, Guillermo, worked there, too. With the household's economy thus assured, and judiciously administered by my grandmother, Uncle Paulino had married an attractive girl, with large dark eyes, who, like him in his leisure time, played the guitar and sang. When we arrived in Mexico City, they already had a four-year-old daughter and a newborn son, who naturally received the affection and care that I had received from Uncle Paulino before our departure for the north, and which he had offered as though in anticipation of the time when he would shower such attention on his own children.

From the time they returned from Zacatecas, my uncles lived on a street in the Guerrero colony. "When we lived in the Tulipán," or "When we lived in Mosqueta," were familiar phrases to my ears, allusions to my fragmentary recollections [of earlier places of residence], reactivated now with our return, of events such as the celebration for Uncle Samuel, which I barely managed to capture. I suppose that they lived in that neighborhood because of its proximity to tram stops, and easy travel to the offices where my uncles worked, and because doubtless it was populated by the aspiring, "decent middle class." Aunt Virginia, however, who always breathed finer air, lived in a San Rafael district that then seemed more aristocratic, possibly because it was farther from Guerrero, whose streets at night were full of stokers, train conductors, and the typical crowd that congregated around the Salón Saturno, the billiard halls, the Vicente Guerrero and Briseño cinemas; on the streets of San Rafael, near the new houses in that style called *mission*, one could see the North Americans she adored, whose language she had learned on her own, and one of whom she had married, an adventurer who disappeared, leaving her with four children, and even though he asked her much later to join him in Havana, my mother never approved, and never let my aunt forget it.

The Sunday following our arrival, my grandmother gathered everyone in the family around the table. I was very disheartened to meet my cousin Fred, who was older than me, but ugly, rough, and crude. His sisters were much nicer. Lilly, the eldest, was very gay, and after the meal, when we had gathered in that carpeted room with red furniture and gilt mirrors, and my uncle Salvador sat down to the piano, she tried to teach me to dance. I couldn't follow those rhythms I'd never heard of—the fox-trot, the one-step, the two-step—that were all the rage, but which to me were totally strange. In Torreón, Uncle Francisco had had among his furniture a kind of cabinet, which by means of large, perforated metallic disks, produced a sweet, soft music, of which "La Zarina" was a song I remember. My father had once bought me as a toy an apparatus, whose name I never knew—it had strings that were attached horizontally and a little keyboard that when you touched its keys, operated slender, laminated metal hammers. This little machine came with a notebook with a few playable pieces, and I learned to play them, because it was as easy as beating on a drum. Anyway, even though the industrious Pane Kypurós never managed to finish the piano whose keys he carved and polished, he had a phonograph with recordings of Caruso and songs sung by María Conesa, whose sharp notes could pierce right through the wailing of Basilio, of Jorge, and of Mague, the newborn baby girl. But aside from those musical fragments, what my ears most remember are the songs sung by that blind man strumming the guitar on the corner at La Sencilla, the miserable little storefront belonging to a leprous Chinese, or the revolutionary folks songs that wafted out from the shacks—"Valentina," "Adelita" (which one of our dark, robust house girls bragged was named for her), the "Pagaré," or "a song of Guaymas, in the style of Mazatlán"—or even the serenades I heard sung, when I was in bed, such as the airs of "Alejandra," floating above the street as an offering to some girl. At the time we were leaving Torreón, a song was becoming popular (and its melody is strongly associated with my memories of the episode at the Hotel Washington) that spoke of "the little birds in the branches that fall in love." I also remembered many bits from the operettas that traveling companies used to bring to the Carpa Pathé, and which I'd go to see on Sundays with my father: María Caballé in *La casta Susana* [Chaste Susana] and in the *Princesa del dólar* [Dollar Princess] and even something as new and sumptuously produced as *Las musas latinas* [Latin Muses].

But these new rhythms took me by surprise, and I couldn't dance them. "Pretty Baby" was the biggest hit, along with another I think was called "Mucha mostaza."[13] When, a few days later, they took me to be registered at the Preparatoria, and I heard the doctor dispatch me quickly with the sentence of "flat feet," I was looking down over the railing of the third floor at the patio where the boys were dancing and making a racket while the orchestra filled the air with the notes of the first big dance party I'd ever heard.

In our first days there, Mexico City showered me with infinite pleasant surprises. Large, clean, and with clear air, the city let one admire its old buildings and the Porfirian constructions not yet profaned by the ax or replaced with skyscrapers. Traffic was moderate, in keeping with the population; pedestrians strolled safely and leisurely through the streets, and crossed without hurry or fear. I was taken to Avenida Madero—to the Regal and High Life stores, which later consolidated as the High Life—to buy a dreamed-of pair of shoes with white rubber soles. Parading their distinguished, decadent indolence, the *fifís*, or dandies, multiplied like the daring mannequins in the windows of Bucher Bros., the tailor shop at the corner of Bolívar and Madero that set the tone for masculine elegance, and advertised its styles in the stereotypical drawings of Carlos Neve: tight, high-waisted trousers that showed light-colored hosiery, or elegant gaiters, and walking boots with rubber soles, short, tight jackets with a vent in the back, very wide lapels, and a single button. The hat, reproduced in a popular advertisement of the day, showed a smiling old man wearing a worn-out hat, saying: "If my hat were a Vencedora, by Lino García, it wouldn't be all broken down"; while another ad, also by Carlos Neve, disputed the primacy of La Vencedora by declaring, "From Sonora to the Yucatán they wear Tardán." The hat was an indispensable accessory and garnered a great deal of attention—one had to follow changing styles in the width of the brim, or the position of the ribbon, or the form of the crown; but the season ended with a sudden and absolute uniformity, come February 10, when the "baskets," or straw hats, appeared triumphantly on the store mannequins and on the head of every gentleman. Thus, the dictatorial model of masculine elegance, established by Carlos Neve and supplied by Bucher Bros. via La Vencedora, Tardán, or Sanjenis, passed from art to become life; stereotypical advertising images got translated into the bearing of those *fifís*, who stood firmly supported on their left foot, and perhaps leaning on a cane, the right foot languid, as though beneath the imaginary train of an evening gown worn by a *prima donna*, their faces radiant and powdered, their eyebrows plucked and with the hat pushed back, as style demanded.

Our lives soon returned to normal. Once our furniture arrived from Torreón, we moved to a small house around the corner from my uncles, who proposed that my father remain in Mexico City, and they found him a night job with the railway. But inexorable circumstances—of which there were many—were already pushing my father to return to Torreón, not that he was running away from us, but rather expelling himself from us against his will. My mother, now certain of her family's support, treated him sternly, coldly, and with hostility. His health worsened, and far from this being a reason for her to surround him with tenderness, it justified her imposition of an increasingly rigid quarantine—at meals, in his bedroom, and in the repeated prohibitions about his so much as touching the textbooks my uncles had hastened to buy me. So he returned to the north, alone, as he did six years ago; but now he was sick and barely able to overmaster the weak illusion that he was leaving behind a son who seemed not to love him very much, and who this time would have no reason to follow him; this canceled out any need for my mother and me to live on our own, and in the precincts of my grandmother a space opened for both of us that would meld us into that family: I was afforded the status of younger brother to all my uncles; my mother's authority was overmastered by the supremacy of my grandmother, who set the tone for the ways in which each and every one of my aunts and uncles reacted to my withdrawal into the inhibited, artificial, conditioned realm of adolescence.

While before our exodus I had the treasure of my aunt María's tender affection, during our absence her preferences got transferred to Estelita, Paulino's daughter and now the spoiled favorite of all my aunts and uncles. And though Julia at first renewed the happy friendship we'd begun during her visit to Torreón, it lasted only a short time. Her constantly deferred marriage, her bad health, which was increasingly resistant to any treatment, made her bitter, neurotic, explosive, and increasingly hateful toward my mother; she was openly resentful of the fact that my mother was healthy and robust but also useless and ignorant; that she hadn't attended the advanced schools where she, Julia, had studied; that she didn't know how to embroider, sew, or weave, nor (as she still did twice a week) had she taken piano lessons; not only had my mother undeservedly gotten married, but now she, Julia, had to accept that she was being reintegrated into a family that should no longer be hers, that my mother had come to usurp her place in the family and as my grandmother's favorite, as well as in the household economy, the place that Julia felt was hers by right of her maiden state and the precarious health where her frustrations always found refuge.

Once our cohabitation with the family became established and routine, she soon fled from the commotion of gifts and outings that filled our first days, in a show of indifference, the clearest definition of her many moods, and barely aware of the negative effects on me. While my mother shared a bedroom with my grandmother (which incited Julia's jealousy even more), I slept in the dark room of a Guillermo who was now an adult and, consequently, spiritually absent from a house to which he barely came to eat and sleep, after evenings spent in movie theaters with his buddies and some sluts. His bedroom led to the dining room, whose table was extended in order to define set places for my mother and me. Occupying the head of the table was Manuel, the doctor, whose arrival was always causing a delay in the rituals of dinner and supper, and whose hard, rather squinting gaze and brusque, authoritarian ways began to fill me with anguish, with the humiliated terror that I would be guilty of involuntary errors of etiquette, or unseemly excesses in the amount of food I consumed. Manuel shared with Salvador the contiguous bedroom, beyond which was the mysterious, to me inaccessible, room for his medical consultations, perpendicular to which was the patients' waiting room, whose glass walls were all painted white, and which was also the antechamber to the last room—the one with carpets and red furniture—where Uncle Salvador, who returned early from his work, played popular songs on the piano with his wide, flat hands, dreamily and "by ear," for though he had shown musical talent even as a child, it wasn't possible for him to study, since he had to go out to work at such a young age.

The indifference that cooled the initial warmth of my aunts and uncles' welcome seemed to signal that I was no longer a child but was becoming a man, one being granted a special privilege, for which I should thank them, namely the opportunity to prepare myself for a life that they had not been able to enjoy. If now they no longer took me on outings, or even barely conversed with me, it had to be because they supposed that my time and attention were to be focused on my studies, given that only through education, and my own effort, crowned by my earning a degree, would the opportunity arise for me to support my mother as they had done for theirs, but their generosity granted me the best conditions to achieve this emancipation.

My uncle Paulino, who, despite having married, continued to be the family mentor and spent every Sunday with my grandmother, offered me the leftovers of the affection he now devoted to his children, and gave me money for movies and books. Providence seemed to have begun to reward his rectitude and spirit of youthful sacrifice. A close friend and godfather to a railway worker—Paulino Fontes—who was a very close friend to President Carranza,[14] helped hasten his advancement. His wife, the beautiful girl who sang with such passion the Spanish songs she played on her guitar, took on a new elegance, wearing furs and jewels, and a collection of birds-of-paradise feathers whose many colors framed, like grand parentheses, her round face and large dark eyes. And when thrifty Uncle Manuel acquired the ability to visit his clients more often with the purchase of a 1917 Ford two-seater, my uncle Paulino surprised us by unveiling a magnificent Hudson Super Six, with a chauffeur, as well as two houses, one of which—sumptuously and immediately furnished by El Palacio de Hierro [The Iron Palace]—they moved to, while they rented the other.

The classrooms of the first-year groups at Preparatoria were separated, prudently, from those of the higher grades, in what was called the Saints Peter and Paul Annex. I did not realize then what was happening in that very moment to [our system of] education, which was suffering the repercussions of the alterations, imbalances, and regressions provoked by the Revolution. I was not aware that what we had was not a University, frozen since the times of

Don Justo Sierra,[15] and that only later would be timidly resuscitated by José Natividad Macías,[16] to be reborn with Vasconcelos;[17] I did not know that what we had was the fiefdom of a Department of Public Education conquered by activist *normalistas* [graduates of the Escuela Normal, charged with training and certifying teachers], who awarded themselves the Preparatoria classes previously taught by the Scientists [graduates of the Facultad de Ciencias]. A picturesque *normalista* by the name of Enrique Olivares, who shaved between his eyebrows and dressed in the latest style from Bucher Bros., was, shall we say, the autonomous director of that upper primary school that comprised the first year of Preparatoria. The geography, grammar, arithmetic, and history teachers were all *normalistas*. The few Porfirian survivors included the voluminous presence of Dr. Jesús Díaz de León, who taught Greek and Latin roots from his own Bouret[18] text, and who I—awed to find that he was, in flesh and blood, the author of one of the books I had read without much interest in Torreón: *The Immortality of the Soul*—once approached before class to let him know that I had read him before meeting him, and to broach the subject, asked if the soul really was immortal, only to receive his brusque, "That is not a question to be asked in a school corridor," which instantly turned me against him.

That going from one room to another every hour for a different class with a different professor, in the hurried ruckus of boys parsimonious with their time and slavishly obedient to their studies; and the fact that they kept the door to the street locked and guarded by the irascible [fellow named] Chicloso turned my school day into an interminable and uncomfortable prison term. Between school and home stretched the wide, seductive, unknown city, beckoning me to explore her, to experience through her the enjoyment of my undiscovered freedom. I barely had any interest at all in my drawing classes, of which there were two, constructive and, I think, decorative, the former taught by a Professor Centeno who was about to receive his engineering degree, and the latter by Don Fidencio Nava, who made us draw flowers in vases with colored chalks on gray paper. As often as I could manage it, I fled from the physical and military exercises loudly commanded by a comically corpulent officer with the big mustaches of a circus performer, who made us march around the patio three times a week in the afternoons.

Without surprise, and on a platonic plane not without its own captivating, mysterious qualities, I discovered that Jorge González had also come to Mexico City and was also studying, although in a different group of first years, at the Preparatoria. We spoke, of course, but only a few times, and about trivial things. He knew about my vice, and even insinuated a resigned, half-hearted right to exploit it, rather like a derisive lover who later visits the prostitute he could have married. Perhaps, in honor of the memory—a memory that so rapidly got stale and congealed—I would have acceded to his extemporaneous demands to settle a tacit commitment. But beyond my sincere lack of interest in him, and in the entire matter, which for me was over and done with, two circumstances impeded it. In the first place, if in Torreón Jorge had no propitious hiding place to take me to, his chances were even less in Mexico, a city he didn't know, and where it didn't even occur to him that we could have taken advantage of the Chapultepec Woods, which were then remote and solitary. In the second place, he soon stopped attending school. He lived with his grandmother—I knew now that he was an orphan—in Tacubaya; and once when he was returning home on the tram, he suffered an accident that would leave him lame for the rest of his life.

Among my classmates, I struck up a friendship with David Niño Arce, at first owing to the contiguity of our last names, both of which began with an *N* on the professors' class lists, and then on account of deeper affinities. Although he had been born in Veracruz, he grew up in Mexico City, and knew the place well. After losing his mother, his father—a peaceable judge with the kindly demeanor of a schoolteacher—had reconstituted his household with two of his sisters, schoolteachers who adored their slight, brilliant nephew. They had dark lodgings in an enormous house on Calle San Jerónimo, to which David brought me one day to introduce me to his family, and to show me the many theater books that filled the two or three irregular bamboo shelves in the room whose furnishings were protected with lace doilies from the sebum of human heads. With this boy I started to skip school—certain that with a few days of intense application I could pass the tests—to play hooky in favor of going to Chapultepec, the Alameda, the Museum, or to explore downtown, go window-shopping, or to taste the sweets that were unknown in Torreón (where the limited imagination of the local confectioners yielded only the monotonous offering of soft, fat candies "filled with hazelnuts and coconut") and on which we spent our weekly tram allowance. I was immediately drawn to the luxury, to the exquisite qualities of this city. And my desire for them made me want to share their discovery with my mother. I thought of her as I stood before each beautiful shop window; in my imagination, I dressed her in the fancy outfits whose display I admired; and some weeks I saved from my allowance the money I would have spent on sweets, to give myself the pleasure of surprising her with the unexpected gift of a black and white hat with *aigrettes*, which I had staked out for days in a shop window, afraid that it would be sold before I had saved up enough to meet its price.

I soon ended up systematically missing school. Classes were held only in the morning. Since I was not in the habit of keeping current with any of them, I put off returning to them all, and started going on regular excursions with David, fearful about not knowing how to answer if I should be asked at home about classes. In the afternoons, I installed myself in the Vicente Guerrero Cinema. At the time there was an intense vogue for hair-raising serial adventure films. I didn't manage to see *Mysteries of New York* because they had shown it before our arrival, but it had the honor of being printed in a series of notebooks that I devoured, stretched out on the black leather furniture in Manuel's vestibule where the family kept most of its miserable little library, on mismatched shelves that also held pieces of crystal: textbooks, such as Ganot's *Physics*, which the doctor had kept from his coursework, or frivolous French novels that at night he left lying around in his office, and the poetry and translations that Guillermo bought: Felipe Trigo, Zamacois, Anatole

France, Marquina, Rubén Darío, Emilio Carrere.[19] From my open reading of these books, I took away more than one consideration: first, that there would be books that I should not suppose I could read without falling into sin; second, that—like everything in that house—the books were not mine; and then, that my reading should not be extended beyond my texts for class. So it was that the cinema, and not my early reading, became my evening escape and the refuge for the loneliness I knew so well. The Vicente Guerrero was basically a shed with uncomfortable seats, where everything smelled of the urinals, and the total silence of the films was punctuated by the notes played on the piano by an old, virtuously dressed señorita, who seemed to be practicing her next day's lesson with extremely languid waltzes. I would sink into the exciting and seductive delight of that darkness in which the luminous screen kept presenting, parading, itemizing, aggrandizing all those beautiful characters in the films. The nobility, strength, and bravery of the heroes worked in me, germinating an adoration of their mythology, and little by little, I discovered with astonishment that I was in love with one of those heroes. When the final close-up homed in on his strong bare arms around the girl, and he sealed her lips with his own, I substituted myself for her, not for him, so as to savor the delectable, warm, moist contact with his mouth. That passion obsessed me, that desire infused me with anguish, given the impossibility of its ever being fulfilled. When I thought of that hero, when I trembled with love while watching him on the screen, what made me suffer was not the thought that his real-life person was so far out of my reach. For me he was there, that *cowboy*, with those clothes, with those arms, with those gestures and those eyes. What separated me from him was simply and tragically the fact that I was a man as he was, and not a girl, like the ones he was kissing, and for whom he performed the most exceptional, heroic deeds in order to save them from villains and claim their kisses. I was humiliated, not by the thought of being *abnormal*; not by the fact of feeling for this man a desire and a passion that I was incapable of condemning, of considering as culpable; but rather by the fact that my feeling was without a doubt so singular, made me so unique, so strange in the world, that if my hero were to know of it, he would probably feel nothing but contempt for me, would humiliate me, hit me instead of kissing me.

And so through the mythology afforded by cinema, I was roused to live a whole complex series of experiences that made manifest, that crystallized, my developing character: with its search for pleasure in suffering, in exaltation through humiliation. I thought of writing a long letter in which I would confess my love and ask of him, offering, if need be, my very life in exchange for its culmination in one precise and glorious instant, a single kiss.

Sometimes, however, Guillermo persuaded me to go to the other cinema, the Briseño, where he was often seen with friends of his own age, or with whores. There, at around seven in the evening, a loud and famous orchestra displaced the pianist, and elicited an intense attraction for the supposedly sensual dances that were its specialty. But that was not my ambience. Thrown together with the whores, I was inhibited, frozen, I didn't know what to say to them, and Guillermo, for his part, dared only introduce me as his "nephew," leaving me the initiative—which I never took—for any subsequent consummation. Among his friends. since their childhood, was Carlos Dávalos, the son of Pacecita, an active, manly woman who wore a pince-nez and who, armed with an umbrella, divided her time between two professions: midwifery and piano lessons. Pacecita had brought me into the world, and everyone says it was she who managed to teach me, no longer a small child, to roll the *r*. She forced her son Carlos to learn the piano by frequently beating him, when she and her children Carlos and Alicia were living in a wing in a house in Guerrero, where the other family was my grandmother's. My uncles many times were indignant when they saw with what cruelty Pacecita hit her son, although later, upon learning that the young man was a real devil who literally kicked his mother around, they came down on her side. Carlos, about the same age as Guillermo, was his schoolmate, and now they and their other friends met in the Salón Saturno or with the whores at the

Briseño. And one evening Guillermo came home with the obvious signs of having been in a fight. That night, as we were sleeping in the same room, I dared to ask him what had happened, and he told me laconically that he had fought with Carlos Dávalos, and that he would have nothing more to do with him, because it turned out he was a whore. I didn't look any further into this incident; but listening to Guillermo condemn Carlos, I felt myself turn red; that such contempt, that the violent rupture of a long-standing friendship stemmed justifiably from the same sinister crime of which I knew I was the defenseless criminal; and that life held for me the same fate—of being the abject, sudden, and irremediable outcast—when each one of those normal, well-balanced beings who had girlfriends and caressed whores found out that I, on the other hand, breathed life into an anguished, unquenchable thirst for the kiss of a cinematic hero.

Around the same time, the inopportune arrival of a letter from Pedro Alvarado, which my mother opened before passing on to me, aggravated my emerging guilty inferiority complex with her inquisition. That dunderhead had come to the railroad station to see me leave for Mexico City, but my parents hadn't noticed his presence there. Now with this loathsome letter—what he was writing me I barely remember, most of it was incomprehensible—my embarrassment was focused on the paragraph in which he announced that he might soon be coming to Mexico City, and looked forward to enjoying again what I'd brought him before. "What had I brought him? And who was this who was writing me in such a way?" I had no idea how to answer, overwhelmed, naked, stained, and guilty, annihilated by my mother's hard, cold, inquisitive gaze.

From then on, the bitterest sense of defeat took control of me, generating an escapist will toward ruin that found its anguished release in masturbation. I didn't arrive at its discovery through pleasure, but rather (as the first, unprovoked ejaculation did) through a recurrent anxiety without tumescence that impelled me to seek the calming spasm as an escape and a compensation for my frustrations. And so I added another disgrace, an extra sin to my daily repertoire of faults: from hiding that I didn't go to classes, to my betrayal of my uncles' trust and generosity, to the crime of ardently desiring the kisses of an actor on the screen. That activity, as usual, and as all sexologists know, imprisoned me in a vicious circle of repeated wrongs and sterile repentances, apt to darken to my eyes every horizon, grotesquely magnify all obstacles and chain me to them, a prisoner of a totalizing will toward ruin. The school year was drawing to a close, and against all my most optimistic intentions to catch up to my classmates in their studies, it was no longer possible to manage it, or even to try somehow to scrape by. The strict *normalistas* had forged a regimen that didn't allow either genius or improvisation. A 10 percent rate of class absences meant that one lost the right to take the regular exams, and I had far surpassed that margin. Overwhelmed, feeling the earth fall away from my feet, I went to the secretary of the Preparatoria and begged, implored him to make an exception for me, and let me sit for the regular exams. This Professor José Manuel Ramos was a desiccated, yellowish fellow who enjoyed demonstrating how energetic and inflexible he was. And so, when I pressed and begged, he asked me, loudly, what my uncles would think: "Don't act pathetic," he flagellated, "because it doesn't get you anything."

I could not measure the magnitude of sudden hatred that that phrase made me conceive for that teacher. A hatred of all my blood, all my powers, swearing to take a blind, annihilating vengeance against that miserable wretch who, without leaving his office, and without a second thought, could inflict such damage on me. A hatred such as I have never felt for anyone; ten years after that episode, when I started teaching a literature course in a secondary school, I haughtily quit upon learning that Professor José Manuel Ramos was the director of the school; and thirty years later, even though he may already be food for the worms, I am not sure my hatred has been completely extinguished.

So I had to spend the two months of vacation locked in my room, preparing for the special examinations in all the subjects I hadn't studied during the term. The discovery of my fraud froze the already tepid affection of my uncles, who now barely spoke to me. In my halting memories of that period, their faces fade to the background and are superseded by that of my grandmother. Cold as she was—severe, forceful, incapable of spoiling or showing affection to anyone—she yet confronted my case with the tolerance of supreme authority, and made clear that the importance and gravity of my wrongs was within my reach to emend if I were to pass the special examinations. She made sure I ate well, sat me by her side, and redirected conversations whose allusions could wound my sensitivity. On Sundays she made me accompany her to the nine o'clock Mass in the beautiful San Fernando Church. While she prayed the Gospel from memory (and this was the important thing, given that attendance at Mass only counts if one arrives before the reading of the Gospel), I got reacquainted with the altars of that church they had brought me to when I was small, and rising in the vapors of my memory were fragments from the choirs and ceremonies that consecrated a group of *kindergartners* to the Holy Child of Atocha. "Remember that I have promised to listen to any supplication from the heart"—said the missal—"and shouldn't the supplication you make of me concern those your heart especially loves?" So then I asked, with all my heart, for the restoration of my family's affection, good health for all—and money, a lot of money. I retied the commercial knot of a religion of give-and-take, of the bartering of prayers for favors, mercies, and privileges that had been my devotional norm in Torreón; I looked forward to the multiple virtues of an instrument of power without which nothing was possible, and with which everything would be easy. I put my faith in the miracle of getting rich, no matter how it happened, and I left the church comforted, invigorated, by the side of my grandmother, and the two of us would then select the best fruits to adorn our Sunday table, around which all the cousins had to gather. In the evening, while the family crowded into the living room and Salvador played the piano, I went with my aunt María to a cinema that Julia never liked to frequent, because it fatigued her, and she preferred to stay home, together with her big yellow cat of the beautiful tail, embroidering with her slender, nervous fingers one more napkin for the fine trousseau intended for her increasingly uncertain, postponed marriage.

I never got to meet her fiancé, and the only thing I ever learned about him was that he bore the comical name Venancio Chumacero [Mr. Oarlock, in the nautical sense; Mr. Ball Bearing, in terms of mechanics]. In all probability, even though he had asked for her hand, his delays in following through with the wedding caused my strict uncles to prohibit Julia from receiving his official visits, and so—now resigned, now in crises of fury or sobbing—all her hopes of marrying died. She became unsociable, withdrawn. She would hide away in her bedroom to smoke a few slender Gardenia cigarettes, staining those fingers whose perfect almond-shaped nails she had been so proud of once; she looked up the meaning of her frequent dreams in the *Oracular Manual and Book of Dreams*, which gave interpretations based on the magic of closing one's eyes and dropping a pin on the special circle that, according to the number on which its point fell, attributed this or that significance to the dream in question.

Some mornings I went out with Aunt Julia, when she took fresh air or a little exercise. When she was feeling well, after her breakfast of hot chocolate, which she took after everyone else, and wearing her lace cap, and when I had decided to take a few hours off from preparing for my exams, we would walk slowly as far as the Alameda, and I would carry a ball for us to play with. But she was soon fatigued by pitch-and-catch, her mood plummeted, and she preferred to sit on a bench and keep knitting while I went off to chat with David Niño, who had arranged to meet us there. For him, not having the right—for the same reasons as I—to take the ordinary exams presented no problem. His father had just died, and his aunts approved of his abandoning a long course of study in order to follow his vocation for the theater.

It was only then that, in spite of having gone around together all year, David and I openly confessed to one another our identical inclinations. Perhaps we both guessed this about one another, as we recalled certain schoolmates, allowing that This One or That One was very handsome, and admitting that we would like to kiss them. I had to invent my own candidate, because in reality, I hadn't focused on any of those boys. He, on the other hand, had the real-life Benjamín Argüelles; and when David mentioned him, I described a kindly, chubby boy who always went around with Argüelles and who was named Prisciliano Vallejo y Arizmendi. A nervous kid, like a young colt: fair, with green eyes, and a small rosy mouth, with an untamable lock of chestnut hair on his narrow brow, who arrived at our gentlemen's school on a shining bicycle. I thought vaguely that I would like this boy. But I silenced the thought, and named someone else in order to dissuade David from favoring his image, and I also abstained from revealing my consummated initiation with Pedro Alvarado.

When the time came, I passed all the special examinations in all the first-year subjects, and could thus register for the second year of Preparatoria. There was a laughable detail in my French test, which placed the jury in the quandary of committing an injustice if they failed me, and an irregularity if they did not, for it so happened that I both knew, and did not know, the subject matter. As for all the others [the special exams], I had studied by myself; like other students, I had practically memorized the entire *Clef de la langue française* [Key to the French Language] composed by M. Luis Rodier, who examined me himself; of course I pronounced all the words as they were written in Spanish, with clear, emphatic enunciation of each final *s*, and without muting the final letter of *ais* or *ai*. But I wrote everything on the blackboard without a single mistake, and conjugated and analyzed without a stumble. The jury, struck dumb, deliberated. When they questioned me, I answered that I had prepared heroically for the examination, and evidently with the efficacy of all autodidacts who fabricate their own culture; and the Solomonic Rodier adjudged that he had to pass me, given that in the coming year, in the second level of French, I could learn to correctly pronounce a vocabulary that I undeniably knew.

My emendation, and my sincere resolution to study regularly during the coming year, did much to elevate me in the estimation of my family. Moreover, the fact that the prosperous Uncle Paulino and his sumptuous wife had determined to take a trip to New York provided me with the opportunity, in his absence and in company with my mother, to enjoy the comforts and privacy of his house, and to move away for two months from my [other] uncles' overpopulated household. And so I entered the second year of Preparatoria with considerable mental ease, and even with the vain satisfaction of arriving at school in Uncle Paulino's enormous automobile, since he had left his chauffeur at home. There were no books in that house; but its large rooms were furnished at great cost; the living room, carpeted in green, had long drapes and a whole gilded Louis XV ensemble surrounding a marble table on which an enormous bronze lion gesticulated ferociously beneath a palm tree with prominent fruits; its dining room, which displayed china and silver; its warm, perfumed bedrooms, aligned around a small garden between the living and dining rooms, aroused my curiosity whenever I wandered around the house. Aunt Josefina's dressing table and bathroom captivated me with their beautiful bottles of perfumes, salts, creams, paints, powders, and soaps. I woke early in the morning, not because otherwise I wouldn't make it to class on time, but rather to enjoy, before anyone else, the beautiful bath, and to apply, before anyone could see or reproach me, all the creams and all the powders in her abundant cabinets, and to polish my nails with her beautiful ivory implements, and to arrive at school full of vanity, intent on attracting the attention and conquering the admiring envy of my schoolmates, none of whom possessed, or could enjoy, an automobile; and among whom, certainly, I was the only one who powdered his face.

To study, I used to lock myself in the office at the other end of the corridor, where there was a great rolltop desk, red leather furniture, and a typewriter. The house faced the first, but now closed, Calle del Pino, and behind it rose the ugly iron towers of the

Museum of Natural History on Calle del Chopo. Sometimes in the late afternoon and early evening, in search of better light, I would go up to the roof, which one reached by climbing the stairway in the room inhabited by Emilio the chauffeur—a room full of oil cans, and with a basic cot on which he slept. Normally, he wasn't at home during these hours. My mother would be out with my uncle Paulino's small children, whom she took care of, and I remained, absolute sovereign of my solitude and of my vague dreams of luxury and riches.

One afternoon, as I climbed up to the roof, I found the chauffeur resting, stretched out on his cot. I tried not to make a sound as I crossed his room, and went to lean on a parapet, lost in that lovely silence of the panorama of roofs among the trees that looked yellow in the twilight, when I felt Emilio coming toward me, and without saying a word, pressing himself against my body. I turned, and then he held me tightly in his arms, took my hand, and brought it to the prominence rising in the front of his pants. Then he undid his buttons, extracted his penis, and tried to get me to touch it, as he watched me attentively. "Do you like it?" he murmured. I didn't answer. Leaning my back against the parapet, I took it in my hand, more from curiosity than desire; I contemplated its smoothness, the roundness of its head which ended in a tiny mouth, freed of the foreskin that my masturbations only ever managed to soften on my own sex; its beautiful dark color, very different from the monstrous red of Jorge González's, which had frightened me. Slowly we made our way toward his room. He made sure, looking out on the terrace, that no one could come looking for us; he locked the door to his room, and led me to his bed. The pillow, his body, his rough face, his hard hands, gave off an odor of gasoline, which would long be associated with a pleasure I first truly experienced in that encounter.

Upon the return from New York of Uncle Paulino and his wife, my mother and I rejoined my grandmother's household. A few weeks later, a telegram arrived from Uncle José informing us that my father had died, and the letter that followed, with the death certificate and other papers, explained the silence of his last days, during which we had received no news from him. Back in Torreón, he had reopened his store, and in order to acquire merchandise, had undertaken some short trips to the north. During one of these, his health problems had gotten worse, but he didn't want to disturb us. He preferred to reunite in Jiménez with his brother José—there where the three of us had enjoyed, shared, the brief interval of a transitory domestic happiness. And there he had died, his large, sad, green eyes closed forever; his weak, tired body had been buried in that land that was full of trees, where each evening the rains bathed the clear air, which we had breathed together.

The second-year students were grouped in the small patio of the Preparatoria, with a direct entrance via the door closest to Calle del Carmen. Physical communications with the rest of the building, through corridors on three floors, were closed, and the older students used to gather [in those hallways] as though on a boastful visit to the zoo. In a corner of the patio, the gymnastics director, whom we didn't know, had had installed the equipment on which Chango Velázquez and the redheaded Leoncio Ochoa gave exuberantly athletic demonstrations of our physical exercises, which this year were free of military instruction. For the rest, the classes—to which I'd been applying myself since the beginning—became easy and were interesting. We studied French in a sort of amphitheater, with the very author of the textbook, whose enormous shoes and falling-down socks we found entertainment in criticizing. I soon became his favorite. He liked to make us speak, practice, and in such circumstances it was easy to take advantage of noting a new schoolmate in the group, so much older than the rest of us that he already shaved the round face that supported his delicate mustache. Called Alfonso Segura Albíter, he enjoyed showing us a generous paternal affection, was always ready to answer our questions and give advice, to study with us, to lead discussions about class subjects, or other subjects, such as masturbation, whose harmfulness he described as the equivalent of three wasted acts of coitus, and which, of course, he condemned. It was from his sermons, to which normally I paid little attention, that I learned that the ejaculation during the spasm was called *coming*. I did not like him. A tacit competition was established between us, with the advantages of his age and tenacity disputing with my quick and voluble intelligence. And so I deeply enjoyed it when the French professor made fun of him one day when he leapt up to improvise a long peroration on the subject of our required monthly exam and he confused *reconocimiento* (recognition) with *reconnaissance*. But though I had a small circle of admirers, he enjoyed the respect and friendship of the four female students of our year, the two Fernández de Lara sisters—one dark and delicate, the other a rosy blonde with eyeglasses—the slender, blond Juanita Hube; and the mannish, melancholy, strong-jawed María Luisa Vergara, all of whom prudently kept themselves away from the men, sitting together in the first row and sharing their notes. For algebra, we had the option of choosing to study with the rude and drowsy López Aguada, or with kindly old Peñita, who had a comical way of snapping his fingers to hurry us along, was always in a good mood, called us *hijitos*, and was the son of the famous grammarian Don Rafael Ángel de la Peña. I preferred his class for the obvious reasons of his personal kindness, and because it was easier to pass without deepening one's knowledge of mathematics, which was never my strength. The system of monthly exams allowed me to inaugurate a new technique of deception very similar to the division of labor employed by collectives in the general progress toward specialization. My schoolmates who were good in algebra showed no aptitude for French or for Spanish grammar; and since I was the exactly the opposite, we soon discovered a mechanism for mutual aid, whose virtue was that I got the high marks in algebra that they got in French and Spanish grammar. All we had to do was give each other enough time to complete our own written exams—as well as those of our conspirators.

Perhaps the most agreeable class was grammar. It was taught in the afternoons by Don Manuel G. Revilla—Rodilla [Kneecap] we called him, in whispers, on account of his absolute baldness. He scrutinized the class list with his myopic eyes imprisoned behind thick, dark lenses, calling our names in a cavernous voice that seemed to express itself in Greek, which this humanist, we soon learned, actually knew. His hearing was as sharp, as sensitive, as his vision was dim and his character sour. He trembled with horror upon hearing a stertorous "Present!" from the student whose name he called, and asked that we answer in a natural voice. Hugo Tilghmann, who had a guttural voice, full of the dissonances caused by the rages of puberty, he categorically prohibited from speaking, even from answering the roll call, which so irritated Tilghmann that he protested in his most disagreeable voice, sending our teacher into his greatest paroxysms. He only calmed down when I read aloud from chapters of the *Quijote*, to whose grammatical gloss we had devoted the entire year. He was charmed by the way I pronounced the letters *c, z,* and *l* in the Spanish style; and so that I would learn to enounce the double *l*, he recommended that I go to the markets, ask for *avellanas* [hazelnuts], and listen well to the pronunciation of the shopkeepers.

My literary abilities, however, were not coming together. I had brought with me from Torreón the small volume of verses I'd written there, and since then, all I'd written were two anecdotal and tragic poems, which I added, in markedly distinct handwriting, to the blank pages in that notebook of "My First Poems." I regarded those verses as the immature fruit of a childhood already liquidated, superseded, and I made notes all over them, exposing their lack of sincerity, their absence of value, clarifying their meaning and origin, in what was perhaps my first attempt at retrospective introspection. Fortunately, Professor Revilla's affection for me was not born of his suspicion that I had the makings of a possible, an eventual writer. One afternoon, after class, I accompanied him to the hotel where he lived, for he had told me he wanted to offer me a special honor, in addition to the usual prizes for excellence in class work—*Stories*, by Coloma and Valera.[20] I waited for him in the *lobby,*[21] and after a little while he appeared, giving me a copy of a his newly published pamphlet on Common Usage and Erudite Language [*El lenguaje popular y el erudito*], a reply to Don Julio Cejador y Frauca, and which I proudly leafed through to find the following dedication: "To the young Salvador Novo, with the esteem earned by his fine education. The author."

The relative dryness of my uncomplicated studies alternated with my trips to the cinema. In the ongoing battle between North American adventure and *cow-boy* films and the European "art films," the latter appeared to have triumphed. Families discussed, debated, and awaited premières as sensational as *The Seven Deadly Sins* series and other hazy reels starring Francesca Bertini with the chubby Gustavo Serena, or with the romantic Tulio Carminati. In her *close-ups*, Pina Menichelli defined the fatal batting of the eyes, the lips half-open with desire, that young women of the time took to imitating in their own gestures. But this world of dreams, whose style dethroned my audacious, muscular hero in favor of a Febo Mari with his sheeplike face, was for me the equivalent of men admiring and imitating women. I found myself handsome; I smiled at myself, contemplated myself, and began to tweeze my eyebrows. I would go out, hoping that someone, entranced, would discover my aptitude for working in films; and many times, on the way to school, I was on the point of entering what I supposed were the Germán Camus studios, on Calle Mina, to suggest they hire me. Later, this desire to act, which was a kind of magnificent reproduction of my theater games in Torreón, took the humorous form of acting out the most famous cinematographic scenes of the time with Teresa and Josefina, the two orphan nieces of the old landlords of the house where my uncles lived. These two survivors of *porfirismo* hid their faded sterility in the upper story of that house on Calle Guerrero, where we occupied the first floor. Almost immediately past the entrance door, a straight flagstone banistered stairway led up to their rooms. We hardly ever saw them. Don Emilio passed the day smoking, alone in his room, wearing his discolored dressing gown, his white head covered by a blue silk cap. Doña Lupe, the girls' aunt, only went out to attend Sunday Mass, and might appear, very early in the mornings, to water the flowerpots in her corridor and to make sure the cages of her singing birds were clean. Tere and Jose's visits enlivened the solitude of those old people, at least for the few days of vacation they spent with them. One of those times, the family upstairs paid us a visit, and the young women and I forged a friendship; in the late afternoon, when I returned from school, and my uncle Manuel's clientele was no longer occupying the waiting room to his office, so that I could sit and study there if I wasn't going to the cinema, I would go up to visit them, and we would explore the enormous faded bedrooms, even entering the room that was always closed and that we opened as though violating its sleeping secret, as we happily acted out selected fragments of films that they, too, had seen, with grave risk to the stability of those feeble, moth-eaten, medallioned sofas and the curtains from which it was necessary to hang in order to give dramatic emphasis to our incarnations of Lydia Borelli at the moment of her tubercular agony.

Pedro Alvarado made good on his announcement to come to Mexico City. One afternoon, as I was coming out of the house on my way to school, he was waiting for me on the corner, accompanied by a soldier, with whom he broke off conversation to come toward me. I could not hide the displeasure I felt on seeing him. I reproached him for his indiscretion, for his stupid letter, and begged him to consider our friendship over and done with. He insisted that I meet him after school, in the hotel on Calle del Seminario where he was staying, and promised not to attempt anything I wouldn't welcome. So I went to see him. As in Torreón, at just about the same hour, he was waiting for me in shirtsleeves. But my evident coldness diluted any aggression on his part; he seemed resigned, or disappointed, or satisfied not to have to go through the motions of an old exploit. Our slack conversation was a kind of long, disjointed, moribund farewell, lacking any objective. He mentioned that he had come to play baseball with a team from the north, and that in two or three days, he'd be going back. Then, because he wanted to humiliate me with stories of his latest conquests, or to arouse my jealousy, or because our complicity had reached the amicable temperance for secrets that lovers hide but friends find pleasure in sharing, he revealed that he was currently in love with two boys from the Escuela del Centenario: one named Evaristo, whom I had to know, since he had been in my group, and was now working in his father's ironworks; and the other, younger and dark, who was very descriptively named Ángel Gallardo [Elegant Angel].

If his revelations were intended to injure me, they fell far short. The result was that my admiration and surprise were reinforced by the proof that my sin was less singular than I had believed. I was glad that there were other boys like me; I recollected an image of Evaristo, and was sorry not to have noticed his beauty or to have shared the pleasure of his inclination, which I was only now discovering, while I carefully noted in my memory the name of that Ángel Gallardo, whom I promised myself to look up when I returned to Torreón, which it was possible could happen if my mother needed to go there to retrieve what little my father had been able to leave us. Taking my leave, still flustered by Pedro's revelations, I asked him if that soldier with him on the corner was *also*—to which he sadistically added to my amazement by saying that, yes, that soldier was *also*, and, as I would discover, soldiers in particular were inclined to sleep with men.

I had believed everything: about Evaristo, about the other boy; how when he had told me in Torreón that Jorge González slept with motorists, because I knew that Jorge had wanted to do so with me. But this about the soldiers wasn't possible. Of course, I remembered from my childhood, it was said that Porfirio's mustachioed officers wore *corsets* to keep themselves rigid and upright, and that they dyed their mustaches black, and tinted their lips and cheeks with carmine. But that vague memory was only now surfacing in my mind, automatically invalidated by the absolute liquidation of that wizened epoch of *corsets*[22] that no one used anymore, of carmine and white lead powders; by the birth—which until this moment had escaped my notice—of a new type of soldier who combined the ferocious traits of the *villista* in his palm sombrero or cowboy hat, with the less formal, but always virile, khaki or kepi, of Don Venustiano Carranza's army, all of them a clan apart from society, and therefore doubtless free from its various forms of decadence. The most that my reluctance to so suddenly admit to the generalizations that were part of my inclination could accept was that that particular soldier friend of Pedro was as he had assured me, and while regretting that he had not joined us, I restrained the impulse to ask Pedro how I might get in touch with him; I spent days hoping in vain that I would see him appear, alone, on the corner where he had waited for me with Pedro on that afternoon of revelations.

One Saturday, around midday, David came to see me at home. He no longer went to school, and we hadn't seen each other since vacation. But this was a holiday, and he supposed he would find me, and that we could go rowing in Chapultepec, and then go home to eat with his aunts.

I was very happy to see him. I promised myself to bring him up to date on those secrets that were boiling, wanting avidly to be shared, in the small archive of my adventures, since our first mutual revelations coincided with our separation. It seemed to me a stroke of good luck, and a good beginning to the kind of conversation I wanted to initiate, that on the same corner as our house, as though waiting for the same streetcar we were heading for, there stood an odd, singular, attractive fellow, immaculately dressed, his face very obviously powdered, and whose fine eyebrows announced the most professional depilation. "Look," I said to David, gesturing toward him, "how handsome." David looked at me, smiling, malicious, and only later did I realize, triumphant: "He's come for you," he quipped, "he's an actor in cinema and theater." We were already close enough for him to be able to hear those words. We were in front of him, and he gave me a burning, brilliant, scrutinizing look while David made the introductions, and I, flustered, never caught his name. The streetcar arrived, and the three of us climbed on, then transferred to another that took us to Chapultepec, where we walked then sat on a bench, and that strange character exerted on my astonishment a calculated, theatrical fascination; that evening, after taking us to eat in a cheap restaurant downtown, he brought us to the dark room he inhabited, and with his kisses initiated a sad, unilateral idyll, plotted in advance and taking advantage of my friendship in order to deceive me into thinking that this was necessary for the filming of a movie whose great script he had written, and that needed an actor to play the role of the boy, that is to say, himself as a child; a boy who was like him, and who, as I would discover, was like me; who was intelligent, and who would submit to the artistic dispositions of his direction. Indeed the script existed. He read it to me, in his pompous theatrical voice. It was called *Atavism*, and the scenes alternated between the childhood and maturity of a protagonist we both would play: a truculent and terrible drama in the Italian style used in the grotesque, gesticulating films of the period. But I neither saw nor analyzed its defects or inconsistencies. My imagination, clouded over in astonishment, took pleasure in the apparent fact that, for the low cost of tolerating the cold kisses and cinematic caresses of that strange character, dreamed-of triumphs were coming into view. I calculated, designed the costumes that would be needed for my scenes (and there would need to be many, for having just got out of short pants, I had only two pairs of long trousers); I thought ahead to the ways in which I would act in these costumes, it being a given that the film would be a great success. And so, once I had drunk in the whole seduction of his offers; when the anesthesia of his dazzling mirages worked on my sexual frigidity with only the stimulation of his ambiguous, vague physical person, in my mind I transferred the reason for my docile submission, for the enjoyment of a pleasure he didn't know how to give me (or perhaps it was the exaltation of my *I* that impeded the pleasure of my *He*), to the obtainment of a prize that his pleasure—a tolerable cost—would have to provide.

For his part, if that narcissistic character had consciously used the stratagem of the projected film to capture me, he soon forgot the connection between the fulfillment of his promise and my continued concessions, and totally missed that his growing passion for me was met with my own affective status quo. For him, the pretext for our friendship was but transitory, and in his judgment would soon be surpassed by the profound merits of his personality and the growing intensity of his love for me, which meant that I should dedicate myself to him completely, but I was measuring out my tolerance against the increasingly uncertain fulfillment of his promise to make me the actor in a film that seemed unlikely ever to be made. In the meantime, he impregnated me with his sad, anachronistic bohemian life—more Melmoth[23] than Wilde—at least in the diurnal part of his life that I shared. I would go to see him in the mornings, because classes, which started early, left us free at eleven, so I would be present, leafing through books on theater acting (curious treatises on gesticulation, with illustrated plates and diagrams showing the muscles that needed to be used to express anger, or sorrow, or happiness), or play scripts, or old theater programs from his own shows, or his album of characterizations, while he performed the minutiae of his *toilette,*[24] which he always began by shaving himself with a straight razor in front of the little mirror hung in the center of the window, as he hummed and gesticulated, like a singer testing the clarity and strength of his throat, bits from *La vie de Bohème—Chi son? Sono un poeta?—che cosa facio—scrivo—e come vivo—VIVO—,* and in pronouncing that final *vivo*, he would shrug his shoulders and infuse the syllables with all the sincere bitterness of one who truly did not know how he was getting through the days, what with his rent coming due and the meals he took by a kind of subscription at the cheap restaurant where, after he got himself dressed up after his fashion, I would accompany him for a late, frugal breakfast that canceled the need to spend money on lunch. I never knew where his earnings, if he had any, could have come from. Until the previous year, according to what David had told me, he had taught reading and declamation at the Preparatoria. But that course no longer existed, and his efforts to create within the University a School of Theatrical Art, that he would direct, did not seem to have crystallized in a salary. However, he did possess a strong, defiant personality that endowed him with a kind of romantic halo and gained him the admiring friendship of a few women who I suspect could have been his Mycenae, and of others who were clearly his disciples. Among the former were two, at least: the impulsive, nervous Eugenia Torres de Meléndez, dark, with a face full of freckles that screamed out despite her layers of makeup, attention-getting purple clothes, and her hats with black *aigrettes*; and the other, a robust Italian beauty with large green eyes, called Honoria Suárez, who had been chosen to play the heroine in our projected film, and had, it seemed, tried her fortune in the nascent cinema of Los Angeles. There were many others, younger, who were disciples of the teacher Tovar Ávalos, but one among them stood out—Isaura Cano, who was about to graduate as an actress and, thanks to the insurmountable backing of the Master, had gotten a role in Sudermann's *Magda*.[25] Isaura Cano, who felt the profound, irresistible call of the stage, had left San Luis Potosí and come to live in Mexico City with her sister, Isabel, who also studied theater, and with their ancient mother. They had abandoned the facile, normal life in which they were vegetating in a province where their only option would have been to marry for an existence full of privations and ideals they kept hidden; they were like chrysalises fallen to earth from an overwhelming dream of applause, living in the naked room on Calle Argentina where the mother prepared their food on an alcohol burner, and where a few times David and I visited them, sharing their café con leche. From San Luis they received some sort of little pension or income, the amount of which, marshaling their theatrical vocation, their aptitude for egregious simulation, they exaggerated; added to this, aside from the practice they got in cultivating their ease for when they should be on stage, was the pathetic payment—coins, really—they got from sometimes joining the choruses of operas (trying to stay out of view of the audience, which soon enough, would be clapping for Isaura alone). The two sisters were very similar, dark and slender, but Isaura's ugliness was illumined by the intense and tragic brilliance of her eyes, above a full mouth that on her sister Isabel, who was a kind of resigned shadow of Isaura, was thinned to a permanent rictus of anxiety and fear, without any trace of the optimism with which the actress confronted her imminent graduation as a public artist, and anticipated a future certain to be glorious.

The Maestro's other younger disciples were the smiling, ingenuous Teté Tapia and the skeletal Armandita Chirot, who was rehearsing a *Marianela*[26] with the young, handsome Luis Enrique Error, who in Preparatoria had been one of the Maestro's students of declamation and had great oratorical gifts. Owing to his youth and to his short stature, which gave no signs of developing, David was only cast as a child or boy servant in the rehearsals for the brief season in which *Magda* and *Marianela*, along with other "period pieces" such as *The Banquet of Deception*[27] (in which the Maestro would demonstrate his mastery of hysterical laughter) would be performed. And I, who attended the rehearsals and applauded from my seat the entrance of Isaura Cano (launched finally to the stage confraternity under the name, imposed by the Maestro, of Issa), in the beautiful long pink taffeta gown with full, trailing sleeves, lovingly made in the room shared by the three women; and where I admired the impeccable diction of Luis Enrique Error, the dramatic flair of Armandita Chirot in *Marianela*; and only once did I have the pleasure, in a "period piece" whose name I can't even remember, for all my interest was concentrated on the makeup and silk outfit required for the fleeting role in which I appeared, dressed like a page, to say three or four words, on the stage of the Teatro Hidalgo.

Once my uncle Salvador brought a friend home, and they went into the living room to chat and play the piano. Attracted by a brilliant execution that sounded nothing like the heavy dances habitually manhandled by Salvador, I leaned in and saw, naturally, that it was his friend who was playing. I was introduced to him, stayed for a moment, and then left them alone. After a while, they left.

A few days later, the brilliant pianist came to call for my uncle, at an hour when he was not at home. I went to tell him this, but he did not seem surprised. He was carrying in his hand a box of fine candies, which he offered me, and a little dictatorially, invited me to go walk with him for a few blocks.

It was evident that my uncle, perhaps on the day we met, had told him in some detail about my situation as an orphan in his house, as a poor student—such that, either because he was so extremely astute, or because he had already seen me on the street in the notorious company of Tovar Ávalos, or because his intuition helped him X-ray my secret, he approached me from the first moment of our conversation without witnesses on a level of such naked and undeniable complicity, that he left me no time for self-defense or pretense. Nothing, moreover, could have been more welcome or refreshing than the opportunity to have a confidant, so capable and so disposed to widen the world of my experiences. Although at the beginning he was quite open (and, in truth, captivated by the chance to confess, I didn't much notice his reactions to my confidences), he later admitted that he was in love with my uncle Salvador, even though he had little hope of fulfilling his desire for this good man who seemed not even to notice. Ricardo Alessio Robles was from Saltillo. He belonged to a large family of politicians and combative military men aligned with a Revolution that was now triumphant, with its Don Venustiano Carranza having ascended to the presidency, and they were being rewarded with lucrative official positions and diplomatic posts for the ideas and contributions that helped bring about this success. But unlike Miguel, who was a lawyer; or Vito, who was an engineer; or José, who was in the military, Ricardo dedicated to art the passionate talent common to his aggressive family. He had won prizes, and a scholarship to the Conservatory, spoke with familiarity and humor about Fanny Anitúa[28] and other classmates there, recounting amusing anecdotes, calling them by comical nicknames that made him burst out laughing, his mouth—with that full lower lip—wide open. His face, with the deep circles under his eyes, was profoundly expressive beneath a baldness he combed over with a light layer of black fuzz; he modulated his gestures and the postures of his slender, agile body, always well if slightly effeminately dressed, with an operatic grace that was deliberately grotesque, making one forget, completely hiding the virility of his close-shaven beard, when suddenly, unexpectedly, in the middle of the street, leaning on the arm of his interlocutor, he would decide to scandalize the passers-by and send his mortified friends fleeing by launching into an aria from *Aida*, from *Samson*, or from *Faust* in his extraordinary, ringing soprano. For the world who knew his pianistic talent, and for those whom he guided at the Conservatory or in the private classes he gave in the living room of the guest house where he kept a room, he was the maestro Ricardo Alessio Robles; but for the intimates of his amazing world, [he was] the incredible, dispersed, nocturnal, embarrassing, brazen king who inspired fear and loyalty, a world in which he had established the dominion of his overwhelming personality, and where he preferred to be Clara, Clarita Vidal, the nom de guerre that he had chosen for himself, he who with such descriptive acuity forever marked his friends and enemies with cruel nicknames: Walled-In Eva (on account of her deafness); Straining Gasbag, a name that perfectly described the constipated gait of the person alluded to; Emma Moreno, who was excessively *morena* (dark); Annie the Cock (who in deferring to Wagner and Levien by selling their printed music, sublimated her own faded but not renounced hopes of becoming an opera singer); Cushion Cunt, who by night received her friends (selecting them so that Annie the Cock, with whom she maintained a kind of old matrimonial tie full of mutual but mutually hidden infidelities so as not to arouse jealousy) in the tiny apartment that the laborious leisure hours of the government employee had yielded an infinity of capricious silk cushions that were, like the delicate *merienda*[29] she offered, and the large blue floor lamp with gilded fringe and flowers, the work of her own hands.

So Clara, winking, would introduce me as his *niece*, his automatic impulses to disfigure people's names stoking the ferocious, intransigent phobias against the timid inverts who fled the scandal of his aggressive friendship. If he happened to stumble upon them in the street, and they didn't flee in time, he would fill the air with insults, or, letting them fly as they passed by, he would spit out the name he had given them. So it was with one Carlos Meneses,[30] who feigned diplomacy on the basis of his grand lordly airs, which contrasted with his truly minimal stature, and whose little eyes never knew where to look, forced himself to stoically tolerate Clara's screaming, "Cream Puff in a Corset!"[31] What seemed to irritate Clara was not that they were like him, but that they showed it less obviously, or that they withheld the homage and admiration due to him as queen and capricious ruler of his time. And so, owing to his official connections, which gave him entry to the bureaucracy's upper echelons, he would present himself in the offices of his *girlfriends*[32] and gain permission for them to step out at the moment, to go *whoring*[33] with him, which consisted of swishing with him through the streets, brazenly eyeing—and sometimes with immediate results—men whose faces lit up upon seeing them, upon registering the come-hither that would leave them spellbound, and when they signaled desire, he would confront them with a suddenly recovered virility, to ask if they wore earrings, and why they thought they were worthy of such an invitation. With the same insolence, he would appear in the wimpy studios in which India Bonita or Águila de Carrizo sheltered from a hostile, vulgar world by savoring a refinement that consisted of taking tea and wearing silk dressing gowns, only to upset the careful order of their furnishings and break up the harmony of their homogeneous gatherings with his guffaws and arias, or by sowing a nasty seed, or weaving a nasty web, or telling a slanderous joke that would end up distancing those friends, and dissolving peaceable relations.

When he learned about my relationship with Tovar Ávalos, he forcefully reproached it, and undertook that it should end by delivering me to the caresses of true men, for in his judgment, one *sullied oneself*[34] by sleeping with those of one's own sex, like the Collie Bitch, which is the name he immediately and accurately slapped on the Maestro. And so, while he was giving piano lessons in the living room, he installed me in his bedroom with two or three of the bad boys in his transient clientele, one of whom, a chauffeur named Arturito, who drove one of the first passenger trucks to the *colonia* Roma [a neighborhood just west of the city center, in the borough of Cuauhtémoc], I began to fall in love with, which had me waiting long hours on the corner of Tacuba and Brasil for the return of his vehicle, so I could take the seat next to him and breathe, with a delight both retrospective and promising, the emanations of gasoline from his body.

But Clara did not believe in love, or in exclusivity. He[35] preached and practiced tempestuous passion and happiness, and took me every day to meet different picturesque people, to get acquainted with their bizarre ways and homes: to a neighborhood in which the dancer Pedro Rubín was still sleeping on the floor at one in the afternoon, after a night of orgies he recounted with all sorts of detail; to another neighborhood, near Calle Luis Moya, where there was a masculine *casa de citas* [hourly hotel], run by a waiter whose lover slept at all hours in the big wooden bed adorned with a multitude of blue bows, a house enlivened from time to time by a very old Spaniard who wore his hair long, made everyone call him Carmen, and left at night to work in a bordello where the whores were women.

That was, without doubt, the most sinful of the houses we visited. Upon entering the patio full of clotheslines, the women from the neighborhood, and children playing among the washbasins, bathed us in a look of disdain and pitying curiosity. They knew very well the kind of perverted people who visited the mysterious inhabitants in the darkest and most hidden dwelling, where no woman ever entered, and which remained always closed, impenetrable to spies and inquisitions. Beyond a tiny private patio, at whose ends were a latrine and a brazier, the house opened on to two large rooms, one a dedicated salon, with fainting sofas and faded liana wood chairs, and the other the bedroom of the boss and his lover. My presence, my arrival by Clara's side, neither surprised nor interested the regulars of that place. I was just one who was starting out, more or less as they had started out, and they had in their confidences of yesterday, their conquests of the night before, subjects of far greater interest than my insignificant, novice, and well-groomed person, however much Clara took pains to describe me, to sell me, as exceptionally gifted, the one who at his death would inherit the self-conferred scepter and rule this realm of dispersed subjects. I don't know if it happened by chance, or because Ricardo wanted to avenge himself for his failure with my uncle Salvador by making me aware that there were others in my family like me; but one afternoon, Ricardo got the waiter, ruler of that house, to share some secrets, and those confidences hurt me, because they sullied, retrospectively and atavistically, Uncle Francisco for having brought that waiter to his bed in a house they described to me with total accuracy; it turned out that that waiter was born in Torreón, and had enjoyed for a time the favors of that lonely man.

Of course I stopped visiting the Collie Bitch, whose very image, whose affected poverty, and the theatrical trances of his unwelcome passion, all revolted me. And he, to all appearances, was resigned to being abandoned. When, upon seeing me on the corner of the school, he managed to make me accompany him to his dark room, his reproaches, his recriminations, went from the most humiliated supplication to the most intolerable bragging: to my unfavorable comparison with the beauty of a certain Juan Calderón de la Barca who had preceded me in his life, and who, according to his evocative descriptions intended to arouse my jealousy, was a veritable Dorian Gray; to the most inflamed commentary on the people with whom I had now stooped to mix; and, finally, to the vague threat that he would know how to avenge my disloyalty. His impotence, his inability to keep me by his side (the useless mirage of the projected film having already vanished), only intensified a desperation that his egomania transmuted into disoriented resentment. One morning, either because he watched us habitually, or because he managed to cross our path, he followed Ricardo and me along Avenida Madero. Despite the usual audacity with which Ricardo confronted such situations, the attitude of the Maestro must have been so challenging that Ricardo preferred to speed up and quickly enter Sanborn's. The Maestro couldn't go in there, or keep following us. From the table where we sat down to have ice cream, we saw him pass by several times, shooting us fulminating looks from the sidewalk, but he ended up leaving, constrained no doubt by the sense that he couldn't create a scandal in such a public and crowded place; but also, I guessed, defeated because he couldn't even have come in, sat down, and treated himself to the extraordinary luxury of a refreshment that symbolized the victorious superiority of the resources of the new sovereign of my time and admiration.

I was already in the bedroom when, from the dining room, in which place of honor he was sitting down to supper, I was called by the strict, dry, authoritarian voice of my uncle Manuel. A few months ago, he had established his practice downtown, on Avenida Bolívar, across from the railroad station, and now, rather than receiving patients every afternoon at home, he drove home in his Ford to have supper and then went out again.

His habitually hard, contemptuous manner was now charged with controlled anger. Without preamble, he spat out that an effeminate individual called Enrique Tovar Ávalos had appeared in his consulting room to accuse me of walking down the wrong side of the street, that I visited homosexual bordellos, and that he was prepared to prove it. He had made an appointment, for a face-to-face, for the next day at twelve. And if that turned out to be true . . .

I felt, and desired, death. The whole world went dark. The whole arsenal of my crimes overwhelmed in a single instant of absolute shipwreck my total bewilderment. I could barely summon the audacity needed to deny it, to feign indignation, and to accept the face-to-face appointment. I went to bed like an automaton. I prayed for, yearned for death, and in the pacifying states of insomnia, determined that the only way to save the situation was for me to kill Tovar Ávalos. I would go to see him early, earlier than on other mornings; before he even wrapped his hand around the razor with whose minute caresses he always began his slow toilette, while he was still in bed; I would take possession of the razor and slash his loathsome throat and his damned face, until I'd annihilated him, until I'd erased him from this world that didn't have room enough for us both.

This irrevocable decision made, I made it to his door, and called up to the windows. It was his ghost who opened up, bearing on his long face the evident signs of weeping and insomnia. He threw himself at my feet, sobbing. He understood the terrible damage he had done with his accusation; and would repair it with a full denial, all he asked was my forgiveness, my affection, my company. I was his whole reason for living. He had never loved anyone as he did me. He could not renounce this love, could not resign himself to the thought that I, his god, his adorable and adored child, was being perverted to follow the abject ways into which Alessio was leading me. That was why he had talked; that was why he had cauterized the fire of his accusation with the unacceptable risk of my perdition. And he sobbed, pale, begging, wretched, transfigured. In the face of his sorry state, my absurd plans to murder him were diluted into the most indifferent, neutral contempt. Certainly he needed to retract his story, but for him to do so, I needed to pretend that afterward I would return to his side, that everything would be as it was before; that I understood him, thought he was right, and still loved him. We left it that he would not show up at my uncle's medical office. That way, I would maintain that the slanderer had been unable to support his absurd accusation.

At the appointed hour, the doctor saw that only I occupied his waiting room. Which seemed to satisfy him. Having concluded patient examinations in his inner sanctum, he had me enter so he could preach to me about the contemptuous ills of homosexuality—whether he was persuaded of my innocence or was playing along with my strategy, I don't know.

From then on, I never again spoke with the Maestro. This strange character vanished from my life forever, pursuing his Wildean course; much later, he realized his dream of making a film, *El escándolo* [Scandal], and in order to act in it, he believed it essential to gild his abundant hair and to thus defiantly exhibit himself in the streets; he ended up in Los Angeles, California; twenty-two years after this episode, a series of circumstances and travels brought me to that city, and gave me the unexpected opportunity to learn this, and perhaps I will write more about him in the fullness of time.

In the third year of Preparatoria, the doors to the patio were opened for us, and we were given classes with very interesting names: psychology, ethics, logic, literature, physics, chemistry, and trigonometry. Owing to a policy that I did not then understand, the teachers were of varied background and competence. Next to one or the other survivor of *porfirismo*, like the raging positivist Don Samuel García—pear-shaped, gray haired, yet always elegant—or the picturesque Papá Rivas, or Don Ezequiel A. Chávez, who taught psychology with his own translation of Titchener's[36] text, and who with equal facility leapt to offer a history course—the majority of the teachers were graduates of the Normal School, like the director Moisés Sáenz, of whom it was whispered that on Sundays he was a pastor at a Protestant church, and that he was a northerner and brother of an important revolutionary who also had a Biblical name, Aaron.

In addition to being the director, Moisés Sáenz also gave classes in ethics and chemistry. He was tall, dark, and strong, with a severe face and brow, full lips, extremely white teeth, and a hard look in his eye. He had something to do with the YMCA and emphasized physical education and sports at school. Redheaded Ochoa and Velázquez the Cat, gymnastics teachers who spent afternoons in the large patio, invited us to take part in the morning training for some athletic competitions about which I never knew anything more. Two or three times I got up early and went running, and then to have breakfast at the YMCA, and for the first time tasted a breakfast of fruit, cereal, eggs, and coffee, very different from my usual hot chocolate with biscuits.

A few doctors had said that I had the bone structure of an athlete, which was unusual for someone of my size. But an invincible laziness and neurotic modesty about being seen naked annulled any possibility of my opportune muscular development, and inclined me toward the shrinking attitude and limp, languid, graceless posture that have always been my signature. In addition to my laziness, I was saved from physical education by Moisés Sáenz's decision to name as leaders those students who had the highest academic grades. The leaders would simply watch, exempt from the obligation to participate in the sweaty physical exercises.

Recently arrived was a small third group of very brilliant teachers: young men who had just received their law degrees, or who were still students in that discipline: Trinidad García, Narciso Bassols, Manuel Gómez Morín, Vicente Lombardo Toledano. Their classes—full of fresh teaching—were a strong contrast to the tedious ones taught by old Don Ezequiel or Don Samuel, the dull ones taught by Nica Rangel, the neurotic ones taught by Don Erasmo Castellano Quinto—not to omit the stultifying ones taught by the ignorant *normalistas*.

Don Erasmo was a real character. Suffering from paranoia, paternal to the point of tears, he greeted right and left, lifting his bowler like the top of a sugar bowl while from under the region of his hat he extended his timid turtle head, showing a stubble going gray. Then he would retract his head, like a turtle withdrawing into its shell, and in a vertical movement, pull down his hat, which never got brushed. Don Erasmo had a special affection for me. He read my poems and recited to me his own. I soon stopped attending his classes (he taught Spanish and world literature) because I already knew the texts from my solitary reading in Torreón, and Don Erasmo readily excused me. I was simply to take the trimester and final examinations, and he gave me a 10 [the highest grade].

But we maintained our friendship and stayed in touch. He trusted me; and secretly he had me read and correct the student writings that he was too lazy or busy to have a look at, or that gave his paternal generosity a decorous pretext for my earning a few pesos every month—my first literary income. Don Erasmo lived in San Pedro de los Pinos, then a tiny remote village reachable only by slow streetcar. I would bring the boys' assignments to his small house, crowded with books on and under the furniture, and which, after losing his beloved wife, Bella—whom I knew—he filled with homeless cats that he would go out at night, looking like a beggar, to feed and collect in discarded sacks and bring back to his private shelter for homeless animals.

Without my clearly perceiving it, beyond the cloister of the Preparatoria, which, thanks to the Revolution, had fallen into the hands of the *normalistas*, a movement to unleash a protest in the university was being fomented by the young recently graduated attorneys, who were the advance guard or lightning rods.

One afternoon, gathered on the patio, the boys were making a racket. On similar occasions, I managed to flee before anything more happened; but this time, they closed the doors, there were speeches, shouts; a certain Heriberto Barrón, notably older than the rest of us, led the fired-up multitude toward the room where Moisés Sáenz was giving his chemistry class, to demand his resignation. He came to the door pale, ashen. I didn't see anything else. The next day we learned that some mysterious person had conceded to the students the power to propose the new director.

We all loved Don Ezequiel—so cerulean, always carrying books under the arm whose hand, except for his large white thumb, was plunged in the right pocket of his baggy jacket, with his immaculate childlike complexion, his long, yellowish eyetooth, his smooth manners, his affectionate, repetitive dedications such as the one he wrote in my Titchener: "You are called Salvador; may you always justify your name; may you have thoughts that rescue and never injure, never have thoughts that could kill. Affectionately and cordially, with sincere wishes for your true well-being, your teacher Ezequiel A. Chávez."

Don Ezequiel was named director, to the pleasure and applause of everyone. Arriving at his sunny office through a small interior patio was his secretary, a fair, elegant, young man with wavy hair, whose name was Jaime Torres Bodet.

A few months before, I had begun a casual friendship with a boy in the class ahead of me: the fourth and last year, which shared with the third the classrooms off the large patio. I don't remember how we began seeing each other. Given his inquisitive spirit, it must have been he who approached me, having learned that I had written poems that had been published in the school magazine, *Policromías*, where his first verses had also appeared.

We did not have classes together, but found times outside of them to chat; upon learning that he lived at 95 Calle Mina, and I on Calle Guerrero, I started calling for him at his house so we could walk together to Preparatoria, which wasn't far and took us along quiet, little-used streets.

Xavier [Villaurrutia] had a large family: brothers and sisters. They lived on the lower floors of a stone house shaped like a 7, with patio and corridor bordered by iron railings, a living room with two balconies giving onto the street, a parallel dining room, and then the numerous bedrooms. Once he invited me home to eat, so I met his mother, Doña Julia González, and a few of his brothers and sisters. They all played tennis, and the girls were champions. Their brothers had a sort of small bank or financial firm on Avenida Cinco de Mayo, and a few times I accompanied Xavier when he went there to receive his monthly allowance. Little by little I learned that the family also included writers, artists, and relatives who were very wealthy. They possessed originals by Ruelas,[37] which Xavier showed me with pride. I also learned—for he confided, reticently and swearing me to secrecy—that the family had also had conjugal tragedies and pathetic nervous illnesses.

The predilection that Don Ezequiel showed toward me must have induced him to introduce the "distinguished student" to the young secretary of the Preparatoria, a poet, Xavier informed me, who taught brilliant literature classes in another school—Advanced Studies, near our own. Between classes, I began visiting Jaime Torres Bodet. In his office he introduced me to another young poet and friend of his, who seemed always to be there: Bernardo Ortiz de Montellano. By then my family had moved to San Rafael, to a very large house on the corner of Icazbalceta and Altamirano. Jaime lived at 116 Altamirano. After his work at Preparatoria, we used to ride the same passenger bus toward San Rafael. He would say he was going to prepare his class for the following day: Greek literature at the School of Advanced Studies. Other afternoons, when he did not have to prepare his class, Bernardo would call for him, and once they invited me to accompany them to take tea with orange scones at the Selecty—a small café across from the Hotel Iturbide.

One morning I brought Xavier to meet Jaime in his office. Their mutual love of French literature didn't take long to surface. Jaime and Bernardo had already published books of verse—Jaime, *Fervor*, in 1918; Bernardo, *Avidez*, not long after. But the first book that Jaime gifted me with was his annotated volume of texts by Gide, adorned with a prologue sparkling with learned quotes, published in the Cultura series. "Because of this prologue," he commented with concealed satisfaction, "they say my brain is a house of citations."

Gide and Huysmans were two authors Xavier had introduced me to. *Against the Grain* (*A Rebours*) and *The Immoralist*—which today seem to us so ingenuous—shook us up with their revelations. Of course we had also read, with fruitful admiring guilt, *The Picture of Dorian Gray*. The conversation about Wilde was bringing us closer to sharing confidences. I did not dissimulate my inclinations: Xavier seemed not to have discovered his, or he was resisting acknowledging them. Its recognition, or definition, occurred as befit a life reined in by the strictest literary structures: in the letters we exchanged during the last visit I made with my mother to Torreón. I had spoken in mine about the shock of reencountering the vestiges of my childhood; the young men I now saw with different eyes; Ángel Gallardo about whom Pedro Alvarado had spoken, and whom I searched out and brought to my bed, as though—in neurotic vengeance—I sought to change places with my rapist, and thereby see myself anew. Xavier finally confided in his letters the jubilation of discovering himself—and of the hopeless love he felt for Paco Argüelles, the history teacher's handsome son. His letters were very beautiful, and I will never sufficiently regret committing the stupidity of losing them in lending them to the Collie Bitch before our definitive rupture.

For my part, I could also feel the flowering of loving desire for a classmate: happy, athletic, and carefree, an excellent dancer with lots of girlfriends and romantic adventures: Fernando Robert, who fled from my friendship, which inflamed me even more.

My life was split into three parts: home and family, where I was feeling increasingly strange, humiliated, and uncomfortable; school; and the excursions and adventures I was pulled along on by Ricardo. He would introduce me to the most unusual fellows—and take pleasure in their mad flirtations with me. And so one New Year's Day he threw me into the warm arms of a young soldier—Octavio Larriva; and when I confided that I liked very much Pichón Vallejo, a handsome young man who played brilliant, thundering piano in the school's "cultural assemblies," Ricardo maneuvered it so that I got him to accompany me to his furnished room on Avenida Bucareli, and then he left us alone. It was the first, instinctive time that my mouth performed a glad and suddenly expert caress, which filled me with pleasure.

Ricardo left for Europe. President De la Huerta[38] was very good friends with Ricardo's revolutionary family and gave him a pension so that he could continue to study piano. But his complicity was no longer indispensable to me. Having discovered the sidelong world of those who understood one another with a look, I was finding those looks just by walking down the street: Avenida Madero, where, in the evenings, people went for a leisurely stroll. There, always guarding the door to El Globo, with his cane, his gaiters, his silk jacket, his gaze behind his pince-nez lazy but alert, his groomed gray mustaches, was Señor Aristi, called Tight Ass; next door to El Globo was the studio of *licenciado* Solórzano—who, according to Ricardo, sang opera arias (*Ninon, Ninon, que fait-tu de la vie*), and who was called Tamales because he made his conquests by inviting youths to a late-afternoon snack of "a few little tamales and a beer." Along this strip would come Mother Meza, on the hunt for human goods and clients, who never slept with the merchandise he procured for his buyers, the refined survivors of *porfirismo*. He would approach young men, induce them to learn the guitar, which he offered to teach them free of charge—and once in his room, took the measure of their cocks with a tape measure, opening the doors to a peremptory, but immediately lucrative trade with his rich clients.

Mother Meza occupied one of the many large rooms inhabited in that building by others of his kind: Father Tortolero, full of chasubles and church ornaments; Salvador Acosto, who had only a wide bed that was always occupied. There were others, whom I didn't know, who visited him; it wasn't so that I would sleep with them, but so I could pass on to them my own conquests later. But in those rooms I met practically the entire fauna of the epoch: Father Vallejo Macouzet, who was called Sister Demon, who bore the scar from a knife wound on his lip, and was famous for the clientele of young boys who visited him in his Santo Domingo church; Father Garbuno, from Guadalajara, who always went around with Sister Demon; the Devil on the Corner—a Mr. Martell, famous because it was said he had paid one thousand gold pesos to a bullfighter for a private sword thrust—and the *licenciado* Marmolejo, ugly as an idol, who used to keep a special box in the rolltop desk of his law office containing the pillow he would throw on the floor so he could sleep with young men and belch all over them; and Water Goddess, an antiques dealer, married, with grown children and numerous grandchildren, but persuaded that his conquests were all madly in love with him.

There was another go-between: the Swallow. The principal client of this busy and successful procurer of young men was Richard Lancaster Jones. Pale to the point of transparency, he possessed, but did not inhabit, a sumptuous house on Puente de Alvarado, preferring to sleep in the hotel on Avenida Madero where he kept his clothes and numerous medications. In the evenings, he put a fistful of pesos in his pocket and went to the little room the Swallow kept near Guerrero and Lagunillo. The Swallow started rounding up strangers—at two pesos each—until Lancaster Jones exhausted both his powers and the pesos he had set aside for the day. Accustomed to the luxury of the mansion he disdained, to the immaculate comfort of his centrally located hotel, that solitary fellow must have been impelled by an irresistible masochism to seek, in the Swallow's wretched room, sexual satisfaction from the invigorating youth of his victims.

The communicating vessels of that anonymous confraternity led me to another memorable building, now demolished, nicknamed The Vatican. Many others in the brotherhood lived there; but I only visited the "studio" of the aforementioned Cushion Cunt and, with greater assiduity, the apartment of Dr. Enrique Mendoza Albarrán, called Suzuki because his nearsighted squint made him look Japanese.

To Dr. Mendoza's place the Swallow brought Xavier and, for me, Gustavo Villa—the Virgin of Istanbul. Villa was still a student at twenty-four (an age I found scandalously advanced). At Preparatoria he easily became our friend. And once trust was won, the ice broken, and complicity established, he invited us one afternoon to accompany him on a visit. In reality, (the new young Mother Meza or the Swallow) was bringing me to meet Dr. Mendoza, who had heard about the Faun (as they called me)—and wished to sleep with him; but he came on to Xavier, who liked him, and with whom he ended up falling in love.

Suzuki had discovered his sexual vocation very late: already well on in years, bald, and myopic, he was about to marry a former girlfriend from his province. But he was in a hurry to make up for lost time. His urological practice brought him a whole range of sick cocks, whose health he gladly undertook to restore, with complaining ecstasy, on his wide carved wooden bed.

He liked to have company, to have gatherings that were modest and peaceful. He would sit us down at his table to drink cups of hot chocolate with cookies broken in half, or glasses of milk with a sweet; and then he would sit at the player piano and pedal for our delight, telling us about his most recent adventure, breathless with delighted admiration: "A cock like a swan."

Next to the Olympia Cinema was another gloomy old house: one night I was taken to visit a "studio" there. The typical closed-in smell, perfumes that have gone rancid; heavy drapes, low lights. This studio was shared by Carlos Meneses (cruelly known as Cream Puff in a Corset, on account of his ridiculous stature) and Antonio Adalid. I was surprised to recognize the latter as the English professor at Preparatoria.

The Virgin of Istanbul administered his fine blond beauty in a very different circle than the one that Clara had introduced me to. Clara's scandalous, brazen *amigas* were generally poor and ugly: Seed-Spiller, who pulled away before his pimps could ejaculate inside him "because it is harmful"; Fausta, a waiter in a cheap restaurant and an occasional itinerant actor; Pythia[39] and Walled-In Eva (owing to her deafness), civil servants; Pepe the Hat Guy, who dressed in the comic costumes of the Lyric Theater; the Pretty Indian . . . The Virgin's friends were of a higher class, and less obvious. He had been the lover of the owner of a men's clothing store that was very fashionable at the time: Bucher Bros., and knew many gentleman who had money and young, handsome, steady lovers, whom he took advantage of—either on his own account or to enlarge his business. One of these gentlemen was the congressman Ignacio Moctezuma. He lived in the Hotel Iturbide and had for a lover an athletic young man of German origin, Augusto Fink, to whose outsize cock only Nacho Moctezuma could testify.

In his room at the Hotel Iturbide—and in unfavorable competition with the magnitudes to which his steady lover had accustomed him—I satisfied the fleeting whim that Nacho Moctezuma had shown for sleeping with me, the Little Faun.[40] Our pillow talk was, as is usually the case, autobiographical, and I told him that I was hopelessly in love with Fernando Robert. He kindly offered to help me. Somehow, I managed to sweet-talk Fernando into coming with me to visit Nacho. But once we were there, Nacho demanded, and obtained, a legitimate droit du seigneur.

In the same Hotel Iturbide, I visited one morning a representative or impresario of the Ana Pavlova Ballet Company, which was then touring Mexico. He had seen me at the theater, approached me, and suggested—to my immediate delight—that I could be a dancer and leave Mexico with the company; that—at fifteen—I was at a good age to train and develop. He made an appointment to chat about this at his hotel. He was still in bed, wearing blue pajamas that showed his slightly furry chest. Little by little, he induced me to bestow a caress that seemed to me as ridiculous as it was inoffensive: that I bite down hard on his right nipple. That was all. I never heard from him again.

The visits to the wretched rooms of the Swallow or Salvador Acosta for a quick orgasm, and the more social ones to Suzuki's house or to the studio shared by Adalid and Cream Puff in a Corset, satisfied the need for a home, for free and open company in which to share, loquaciously, our secrets. But it still wasn't enough. At the suggestion of the Virgin of Istanbul, we decided to set up our own studio shared by the three most assiduous accomplices: he and Xavier, already steady lovers, and I, free and on my own. The three of us would share the rent—thirty pesos a month, light included—for a large room in an office building, on the corner of Donceles [Maiden Street] and Argentina, very close to the Preparatoria, where we were all in our final year.

It was the year of the Centenary of Independence—1921—and the celebrations were marked by the strident resurrection of ornamental nationalism: buildings resurfaced with *tezontle,*[41] the publication of Dr. Atl's two-volume *Traditional Arts of Mexico*, which sought to exalt *tepalcate*,[42] and which was published by the powerful minister of Industry, Miguel Alessio Robles—Clara's brother.

We were entranced by the exhibition of traditional art installed in the Regis. One painter, by the name of Montenegro, recently returned from Europe, had decorated a pavilion with stylizations of nopal cactus and cactus fruits on green and red flannel trimmed to make a frieze. Hanging calabashes functioned as lights, making the Porfirian candles unnecessary and ridiculous, and the serapes from Oaxaca, Saltillo, and Tlaxcala were as splendid and coveted as Gobelin tapestries and Persian rugs had been in times past.

I enthusiastically latched on to this style, decorating our "studio" with weavings, needlework, and other handicrafts. From the headboard of the couch[43] we hung a small idol with large buttocks, which we called Saint Bollocks; from this "sacrificial perch," he presided over our scenes. And in a touch of extreme nationalism, I employed a small calabash as the most appropriate vessel for the Vaseline required for our rites.

We purchased an earthen tea set, and took tea in the afternoons with thick cookies, fruit of the oven's womb, which I bought from the bakeries nearby, happy to have a home to call our own. We invited our friends to "at homes," and were soon known by our set as "the girls of Maiden Street."

We didn't always have the money to pay our rent when it came due. Of the three partners, Xavier was the only one with an adequate monthly allowance; but the Virgin knew how to handle himself with his modest friends. He brought to the studio a lover—Don Tito Gasco Rojo: a dark, squat old man who owned a pharmacy and a record shop on Avenida Madero. We left them alone. That month, the Virgin paid the whole rent. The next, it was my penitential turn to receive the voluminous, belching visit of the *licenciado* Marmolejo.

The balcony of our fourth-floor studio gave onto Calle de Donceles [Maiden Street][44] across from the upper offices of the Ministry of Industry. I sat on this balcony, looked toward the street. It must have been five in the afternoon. Weeks before, as we were leaving Preparatoria, Jaime Torres Bodet had introduced me to a Central American poet favored by Vasconcelos. With a wave of his white, carefully groomed hand, he had said, "The poet Rafael Heliodoro Valle," and then, with a slightly mischievous smile, "and the poet Salvador Novo."

Heliodoro showed great interest in my poems. I introduced him to Xavier, whose poems he also read, and he published us both in the newspapers where he worked, and we talked with him about Ricardo Arenales, another Colombian poet about whom we had heard horror stories. He was "the man who looked like a horse," in the description that someone made of him. Heliodoro offered to bring this curiosity to the "young men's studio."

His ugliness was to me as immediately repulsive as his incongruous brazen nerve. I asked him if he liked I no longer remember which poet; and "What I like is to be penetrated hard," he said, sticking out his fat, dark lower lip. Then he took out his special cigarettes, gave us each one, we lit up, I sucked in—three times, holding my breath, as he taught us.

He started to recite his poems. I looked out on the street. Time was suspended. The light was white, an absolute white, in the deafening silence.

When I came to, I found myself stretched out on the couch. I was surrounded by the anguished faces of Xavier, the Virgin, and Dr. Mendoza, who had resuscitated me with injections. It was already ten at night. Frightened by their exploit, Heliodoro and the marijuana poet had left.

The marijuana had had no bad effects, however, on the Virgin or on Xavier. Maybe they hadn't inhaled as strongly as I had, drawn as I was to any unfamiliar or exciting form of excess. The Virgin recounted that in other studios, as in the novels of Jean Lorrain,[45] he had taken ether, and it was lovely how, lulled by the sound of bells, he reached nirvana.

Another night—which I now remember we would call Walpurgisnacht—we got together in couples to get drunk on anise. The Virgin had introduced me to a dark-skinned young man—Gaitán—very attractive. He would sleep with Xavier. It was the first time we were being visited by a classmate we had suspected of being a latent, undecided accomplice: Delfino Ramírez Tovar. Bone thin, shy and unsociable, dressed in white provincial style, he watched from a corner the libations, the necking, and the numerous naked dances with which I enlivened our party, possibly because I was still inclined to become a dancer. And very drunkenly, we extinguished the lights, and panted in the sweaty dark. "That left me deaf and blind," a cornered Delfino told me afterward. "But far from lame," we replied.

That testimonial initiation, however, was enough to launch the shy young provincial toward the conquest of his true vocation.

Days later he was telling us about his first adventure, with a Fernando to whose memory he would remain attached for many years. And with his self-discovery came a luminous change of character. His intelligence and talent awoke; he became my sidekick in our musical "numbers," where he would joke, recite, and sing, with a healthy awareness that he was ugly. He rinsed his hair with oxygenated water to give it a blond cast. We baptized him Porfiria—and he turned "The Girls from Maiden Street," our popular trio, into a happy quartet.

The Virgin insisted that—like him and Xavier—I have a friend with whom I might decently be seen. He thought it could be Enoch Paniagua—a refined, pretty young man of the fair, effeminate type; beautifully dressed, an operatic velvet hat topping his ingenuous and slightly freckled face that blushed easily. Little Enoch contributed to the studio's decoration with a few knickknacks, and would visit us accompanied by his friend Rafael Pérez Gavilán—who, in his ugliness, resembled Torres Bodet. They both liked opera, and Pérez Gavilán played the piano. They became part of our lives, which for them were as scandalous as they were seductive; and when I separated from the "studio" in order to set up my own (a furnished room I retained for only a short time: the interval needed to enjoy the quick idyll with a big, pale railroad man), Little Enoch and Pérez Gavilán remained friends with the Virgin and Xavier, and then, one day during vacation, they went to Los Angeles, California—where many years later I met them again. Pérez Gavilán was the cousin of Ramón Novarro, the famous star of the period. They had the illusion that they would profit, in the world of film, from having him as a relation.

The Swallow procured me another lodging, closer to his own: an enormous empty room, with two balconies overlooking the deserted Calle del Pensador Mexicano [Street of the Mexican Thinker]. In a shop, he bought two wooden cartons, which I covered with cretonne—and every afternoon, after class, Delfino and I would go there. "Have the princesses arrived yet?" the Swallow would always check in, "I'll be right over." From the balcony [after he left] we would watch him walk away—straight-backed, important, imposing in his wretched suit, his threadbare derby, the blackened scab between his right eye and cheek. Soon he would begin his rounds. "Have a nap." And then he'd bring in the next stranger.

Other times he would prefer to take me to his room, which, in the context of his poverty, was better equipped. One evening he locked me in there with a guy who had just set off a bomb in the American embassy; ugly, but the owner of a tool so enormous, it was not easy to accommodate him. The Swallow challenged me, and I accepted the contest. Accompanied by several witnesses, he locked me in with the anarchist, left, came back a little while later, leaned his aquiline head in, and asked, "Done?" "Done!" "The whole thing?" "Yes." And addressing the witnesses who were with him: with a solemn intonation worthy of *Habemus Papa*,[46] proclaimed, "The whole thing!"

The studio of Antonio Adalid, once he had separated from Cream Puff in a Corset to set up on his own, was located at 123 Avenida Hidalgo, very close to the San Fernando garden. It was a detached half of a large apartment on the second floor of a comfortable and then modern building. The discreet door at the top of the service stairway opened to a small corridor, on whose left side were two windowed rooms: a kitchenette[47] at the back, and on the right, a bedroom. When it was decorated and furnished to his liking, he invited me over and introduced me to Antonio Chico, or Little Antonio.

Little Antonio was then twenty-eight, and Big Antonio (Antonio Grande) fifty-three. Twice a week, Big Antonio spent the day giving English classes at Preparatoria, and the other three days, at the Agricultural School in distant Chapingo. At around seven he would arrive at his studio. By this time, Little Antonio had gotten up from his siesta, put on his kimono; and, while smoking, with the long cigarette holder between his already slightly stained teeth, he would light the stove to make coffee, and set the round table for *la merienda*, which they would take in the second little room; in time the guests—no more than four—would take their places on the sofa in the corner, and in the medallioned chairs that set off the fine blue English china.

Paper the color of a Gobelin tapestry covered the walls of those two sober and welcoming rooms, with fine old chairs and curtains in good taste. In the corner of the first room, on one side of the window, was a pianola, on top of which was a life-size oil of a peaceably smiling Little Antonio, wearing a velvet cape, on his chest his beautiful hand displaying the cameo in his ring. A few other Chinese decorations on the walls: a blue and gold Mandarin skirt; and on the bedside tables: lacquered pieces that Antonio had had made by the skillful artisans used by the antiques dealers he had begun working with, which testified to or recalled the fact that the two Antonios had resided for a time in San Francisco, California; a couple of Guatemalan *santos*, carved from wood or marble, marked the beginning of a passion for collecting that would later ruin Professor Adalid.

He would return from giving classes, take from the kitchenette a suitable bowl, and go out again. Sometimes I would accompany him: to the Chinese restaurant on the corner, where he would buy some little dish to have for supper. Then, having taken off his jacket, the diamond-studded tie pin on his impeccable stiff collar, he would settle himself in the center of the small sofa, as though on his throne, while Antonio served, in his black kimono, supper and the two ritual cups of American coffee, then offered the etched metal box of violet-scented cigarettes known as Milo.

Between them—he confided—the flesh had long since cooled. Theirs was a friendship that could have been called fraternal, were it not for the difference in their ages, and for its distant origin in an episode that—once one knew it—called up Antonio Adalid's long-ago image and the golden age in which he had lived his youth.

The Adalids were an old and wealthy family in Mexico. The Marchesa Calderón de la Barca constantly mentioned Señora Adalid—Antonio's grandmother—and the family's spread in Goicochea, San Ángel, along with their many other beautiful haciendas. The Emperor Maximilian had named as his groom Antonio's father, Don José Adalid, whom I got to know, and who was reluctant to climb into a car or answer the telephone; he moved, without the cars but with his dappled horses, to his own enormous house at 13 Calle San Cosme—where I would go with Little Antonio every night, to rise at exactly ten for the peaceful ritual of *la merienda*. Antonio himself, and his brothers, had been baptized by the emperors. Don José's legitimate family (for it was suspected that he had one or more others, in accordance with the most accepted and virile tradition of rich Mexicans) consisted of three women: Pita, Tarra, and Toto, and two men, Pepe and Antonio. Antonio had been sent to England for his education, while Pepe learned to administer the family properties and assets.

He returned to Mexico at the peak of his happy youth—and at the peak of opulent *porfirismo*. It was a time when the exquisite aristocrats gave famous parties: although private, they doubtless gave rise to the whispers and scandals of a prim little city: in short, it was the time of the famous Dance of the Forty-one.

Antonio was the soul of those parties: Toña the Sucker, he said they called him, for his affinity for a caress that must have been unusual then, or that Antonio would have practiced with great European skill or predilection. Stimulated by the second cup of coffee, blowing smoke rings from the cigarettes he didn't know how to smoke, but which he held in his chubby cardinal's hands, he laughingly evoked his early-morning group excursions to Xochimilco, by streetcar, all of them wearing blue jackets and panama hats.

There were procurers—the same Madre Meza?—who found boys for the diversion of the aristocrats. One party night, Toña was coming down the grand staircase in the sumptuous attire of a dancer. The whole gathering applauded his grand entrance; but at the foot of the staircase, the mute reproach of two eyes froze him in place. They seemed to be saying: "Ridiculous old man!" Toña turned and ascended the stairs, he abandoned his disguise, and descended to find the beautiful boy who had silently berated him. At that moment, there was an auction for the possession of that very youth. Antonio purchased him.

He, too, was named Antonio. He was not yet twenty.

Whether it was at the famous Dance of the Forty-one, or at another, a scandal broke out. Don José Adalid disinherited and disowned this degenerate son, this stain on the family who fled, disconcerted, disoriented, and invalidated, to San Francisco, California, with a few dollars in his pockets and no idea what he should do. He went into a church, approached the confessional, purged himself of all his sins. "God brought you here," the priest told him. "We need a Spanish teacher at St. Mary's College. I'm offering you a salary, a room, meals, and clean clothes." Antonio saw the heavens part; he began to give classes, having good English from his years in England, and to dwell on his memories in the solitude of his small apartment. He heard nothing, and wished to hear nothing, from Mexico. The place was dead to him, or existed in a nightmare.

One evening, someone called softly at his door. He opened. "Here I am," said Little Antonio. "You understand that from that moment . . . I would never be apart from him."

Little Antonio learned English. They made a simple, free, and comfortable life together in San Francisco. When Big Antonio's mother died, leaving him her forgiveness and a large inheritance, Don José, in turn, pardoned the wayward son. And the two Antonios returned to Mexico. Once again rich, Antonio had no need to work, but he had acquired the habit of doing so. He enjoyed teaching, shouting in class, giving affectionate but stinging and sonorous slaps to the boys. He began to give classes at Preparatoria. That was where I met him, and began a friendship that was never tainted by his trying to elicit [sexual] contact.

So convinced was he of the perfection of his way of life with Antonio that he thought it would be good for me to be settled into a similar relationship: with a rich older man who would appreciate my talent as well as my beauty; who would support me and eventually leave me his fortune. He tried twice to marry me well: the first was with Don Luis Amieva—a tall, bald old man who had been inspector general of the police, and was starting to look to replace the boy then living with him. He liked bullfights; and the night that

Antonio introduced us in his studio, as Don Luis left—wrapped in a Spanish cape—he put a gold *centenario* coin in my hand on the pretext that I should buy my ticket for the bullfight, and that we would see each other there.

The illusion, on his part, that I would be attracted to his wealth did not last long. When we were alone in his house, which was full of valuable porcelain, on the brocade-covered bed, no effort of imagination on my part, of skill on his, could make his bloodsucker mouth—opportunely and obviously free of dentures—in any way arouse me.

The disappointment of my other prospect was of a different order. Don Carlos Gutiérrez Palacios occupied an apartment in a building on Calle de Balderas—which I believe he owned. He lived surrounded by austere furnishings, authentic museum jewels, soberly arranged on the border of the green carpet that covered the floors of all the rooms. His hobby[48] was death. Beginning with Ruelas, painters, illustrators, poets, and prose writers had satisfied his persistent requests that they make him works with a funereal theme. Dry, dark, fine, with a thin voice, dressed in black, he looked like a Hamlet suddenly grown old in the scene with Yorick, his abundant white hair carefully combed and with the svelte cane his nervous hands maneuvered like a magic wand. When Antonio invited him for *merienda* at the studio with the purpose of introducing me to him, he observed, actually scrutinized, me, but without seeming to. We spoke about art. He had just purchased in San Ángel "some ruins" that he intended to transform into the house where he would bring his antiquities. He had no heirs. He insinuated that if he were to meet a young friend, all of his assets would go to him, at his own death; and that before dying, he was caressing the desire to undertake a trip to Mallorca—with the friend he hoped to find.

He showed no hurry to conquer me. After seeing Antonio to his house at 13 San Cosme—like every night, at exactly ten—we kept walking until we got to my door, where he took his leave. The following day a package arrived from the bookstore with his first gift:

Elie Faure's *History of Art*, which we had been talking about the evening before. To thank him, I went to visit him at his apartment; and I returned several times, without him ever having the nerve to touch me. He listened to me, watched me, and smiled. He had bought theater tickets—and gave me mine so that we would meet there, as though by chance; and afterward we would go for a bite at some almost empty café. I found it inexplicable that he would resist our going to the Antonios' welcoming and pleasant "studio." He felt obliged to confess that, supposing I was Antonio's lover, he felt jealous.

His indecision and calm company bored me. I avoided him, pleading other engagements, returned to Antonio's house, and made everyone laugh about the ridiculous jealousy and the absurd reaction of someone who should have been grateful for having been introduced to me. But above all, I continued my independent adventures. Drivers were my passionate predilection: truck drivers, whom I approached to start a conversation that ended with a date for that very night; or the chauffeurs of hired cars in which they would drive us to some appropriately dark or shady spot. One of those drivers on Calle San Juan de Letrán [Saint John Lateran], famous among the "crazy girls" for his sexaggeration, took me to the house—4 Calle Pescaditos—of one Fidencio, who rented, for two pesos, his room with the wide brass bed.

Without my noticing, Don Carlos Gutiérrez Palacios was watching my every move: he repeated (I now realize) the maneuvers of the forgotten Collie Bitch. At his apartment, one afternoon, he received me with hostile coldness. He knew everything. It was grotesque. He wanted me with all his might. He hadn't dared to touch me. He respected me, considered me a god. He burned with the repressed impulse to kiss me every time I visited, but I had never granted, never offered the slightest caress. For his part, he had tried to blot me out with a dirty nocturnal adventure. And that was how he had learned, from the driver whose consolation had debased him, what I, his intelligent, poet child, did with men of that disgusting ilk!

Months later I learned, from Antonio, that Don Carlos had finally found the pure angel who would inherit his antiquities and the ruins of San Ángel. He had gone to Mallorca with the blond German boy.

Antonio had no interest in an intense social life. His studio was more a refuge: the lovely home where, as in San Francisco, he enjoyed, with Antonio and me, the pleasures of good company. But he couldn't prevent—though he would have wished to—the unexpected visits of certain friends: the antiquities dealers whom he consulted in his hunt for some coveted object (the Guatemalan carved *santos* that he collected); the Water Goddess, a hideous specimen; or the very old Señor Valdés, who lived near Lagunilla market, in a house crammed with furniture; or Antonio Peña, a happy bachelor from Guadalajara who had just left his job in the Tax Department, and who with his young friend Pepe Lascuráin, opened on Calle Gante the first antiques shop devoted to interior decoration; or Pepe Alcalde and Chole Abaunza, with his Chinese-mask face, who was starting to deal in antiques in Antonio Peña's shadow. Tall, bald, blond, Chole made the usual rounds along Madero accompanied by the stout, dark Don Rafael Manzo, brother of a brave revolutionary general and owner of a small palace on the Paseo de la Reforma. The pair were known as Nelly Fernández and his Fucking Mother, the name of a comic then in vogue. Manzo frequented, with more effort than benefit, the urinals of movie theaters.

Now and then, the chubby, myopic Genaro Estrada used to appear at the studio; he was then a high official at [the Ministry of Foreign] Relations and would later be minister and an ambassador, which required him to marry. From his position at Relations he discreetly facilitated the entry into the honorable diplomatic and consular corps of the *loquitas jóvenes*—or "crazy young girls" [in fact, young men]—who came from fine families and sought his patronage. In this way he served the cause by assigning to each official legation a pretty member of the confraternity, who could realize his dreams—safe from prosecution and living in the most varied capitals—of circulating among handsome sailors, soldiers, and guards at Buckingham Palace. His protégés were not necessarily his favorites. At night, he used to be seen ambling down The Slip, the cryptically named corner of 16 de Septiembre and San Juan de Letrán, with the pretext of waiting for the La Rosa streetcar, which, after he discharged the official limousine that came with his position, would take him to his house on Pino, whose walls were lined with books, and where on Sundays he received the powerful Alberto J. Pani[49] and certain select intellectual friends to show them what had arrived by diplomatic pouch from all over the world, the latest publications in luxurious editions: the first number and all subsequent publications of the *Nouvelle Revue Française*.

Another visitor to the Antonios' studio was Chavitos. Like Señor Amieva, he had been an inspector general in the police. Small, dark, chubby, he recounted the most incredible anecdotes about Porfirian Mexico: about a very rich and already old gentleman with many sons and daughters who would station himself in the Alameda Gardens and, dropping a path of valuable coins, get himself followed by every barefoot ragamuffin all the way to his house, where, upon being surprised by one of his sons, down on all fours, his white beard on the ground, he committed suicide.

Dr. Land also used to visit them: an enormous, bald Swede with a soprano voice, a masseur and owner of a house across from the Alameda, where he made sweet, terribly strong liqueurs. I once solicited his hospitality in order to sleep with a truck driver I'd just picked up. Dr. Land opened the door, only to disappear as I introduced him as my friend "baldy." But as I was undressing my truck driver, the doctor reappeared with a tray of his liqueurs: he gave a shout and dropped the tray, so alarmed was he, so certain that the big scruffy boy could kill me.

The courses at Preparatoria ended and I had the opportunity to enroll in the Law School. Torres Bodet was already secretary to Rector Vasconcelos, and I saw him a few times, surrounded by that atmosphere in which he would develop vocationally and become more a personage than a person. Xavier enrolled at the Law School with me; but at school we saw each other less than at other more pleasant nocturnal places.

I spent the boring mornings of classes waiting for the entertaining evenings and nights. To kill time, and still convinced (despite the constant flow of proofs to the contrary) of the exceptional singularity of my character, I started to write a minutely detailed and romantic novelized autobiography that I would call *I*. I quickly drafted many pages and, because I lacked my own furniture at home, as well as a "studio" apart, kept them in my gym locker at the Law School. Every morning I would take out my notebook and, instead of attending classes, sit on a bench in the patio and continue my great sorrowful novel. Xavier knew about it, and was alarmed by its rawness, its sincerity, its mention of real names. And in an act that years later he would repeat (a drawing in which Diego Rivera had rendered me in all my adolescent beauty was made by Xavier to disappear; and the original collection of the *Sonnets*, he removed from a drawer in my house), he forced the lock on my locker and took the manuscript. It was as though his violation had stripped me of all virginity and all worth: when later after an argument he returned my manuscript, I destroyed that first confession written at the age of sixteen.

One midday, I was standing in the doorway of the Law School when a fellow, who was clearly not a student, arrived and went in. Dark, with Negroid features, dressed in black. We exchanged a quick look and, intrigued, I followed him into the school. He went into a classroom where a little while later a large group of *yanqui* students arrived. They took their seats. The individual began to give a class on Mexican literature. He spoke about Sor Juana, and while he did so in a slow, mellow voice, he never stopped looking at me, seated though I was in the last row. He posed a question: "What is a gloss?" His students said not a word. "Anyone, even someone not in this particular class," he said, "You . . ."

I answered, he smiled, ended his class. Intrigued, I waited for him at the exit. We chatted as we walked. It was Pedro Henríquez

Ureña,[50] about whose wisdom, existence, and importance I knew nothing. Without realizing it, I gradually became involved in the small group of reverent disciples whom he would teach in his Socratic way: Daniel Cosío Villegas, who was professor of something or other at the Law School; Eduardo Villaseñor, recently arrived from Morelia; the de Selvas—Salomón the poet, who had just published *The Unknown Soldier*, with drawings by Diego, and his younger brothers Rogerio and Roberto. A friend of Vasconcelos, and now his protégé, Pedro Henríquez Ureña had been the soul of the famous Youth Athenaeum, and the satisfied teacher of Alfonso Reyes, whom Xavier admired and whose books he owned. In the University reformed by Vasconcelos, he had founded a Department of University Exchange and a Summer School for foreigners, whose classes were held wherever space was available: in the classrooms of the Preparatoria or the Law School, or at the Undergraduate College, where he had his office with his big rolltop desk full of small papers, notes, and grade slips covered with his perfect handwriting. He lived at 27 Calle Rosas Moreno, one block from my house. Once he was perfectly sure of my English, he engaged me to give a class on Mexican literature at the Summer School. Involved in the publications of *México Moderno*, and in the magazine of that name, he put me in charge of a section called "Reportorio"; he induced me to prepare an *Antología de cuentos hispanoamericanos* [Anthology of Hispano-American Stories] and had it published. In long monologues, while we walked from the University to his house, he probed, instructed, and calibrated me.

He blurted out disconcerting questions: "Why don't you do philology?" Sometimes he had me stay to eat at his house, which was managed by his old aunt, "young Ramoncita": rice with plantains, before the inquisitive looks of his other disciples, who accepted me with a certain reticence.

Of all of them, only Salomón immediately addressed me with the familiar *tú*. The ingenuous executor of a transparent plan to test me, he took me one night, after visiting Alma Guillén, and as someone who didn't care for such things, to see some Czechoslovakian whores who worked the street across from the Cine Venecia [Venice Cinema]. Salomón went off with one of them and left me in the room with the other, who, like Señor Amieva, and with the same determined oral technique, did not manage to overcome my frigidity. But when we reunited at the exit of that shabby hotel, Salomón appeared convinced of my orthodoxy. And the other disciples, from that day on, accepted me among them with greater benevolence.

Pedro left for South America on the intellectual and artistic Noah's Ark with which Vasconcelos executed his ardent Ibero-Americanism. They carried a statue of Cuauhtémoc, editions of the Classics (what great support we got from the *The Symposium*, where all the crazy Greeks talked about their issues under the wise baton of the crazy elder, the philosopher Socrates, who was a kind of motherly pimp!), and Mexican *souvenirs*.[51] The sculptor [Manuel] Centurión and the painters [Gabriel] Fernández Ledesma and [Roberto] Montenegro had already been dispatched to decorate the Mexican pavilion in Rio de Janeiro. Right before their departure I had gone to the Hotel Iturbide to see the painting exhibition that marked the return to Mexico of Roberto Montenegro, whose loquacity was accompanied by the mute dialogue of his scrutinizing gaze: immediately superior, then cordial. He invited me to his studio in the neighborhood of Balderas, where he was going to meet a few of his intellectual friends: Julio Torri, Jorge Enciso, Fito Best[52]—who had just barely begun to notice me, doubtless more on account of my plucked eyebrows than because of my poetry, which they agreed to listen to in that studio with gilded wallpaper, black floor, red-lacquered Chinese furniture, and lightly scented pompoms hanging from lamps whose light was dim.

With the considerable money I had from the jobs Pedro had gotten me before his departure for South America, and now without his vigilant tutelage, my adventures multiplied. An insatiable thirst for flesh, and an audacity fueled by utter confidence in my beauty and my ability to pay for caresses, threw me into the hunt for the type of men I was electrified to discover, seduce, and exploit: the drivers who in the small Mexico City of the time were of the young generation that drove cars and lived fast.

One day there appeared a newspaper called *El Chafirete*: intended for the guild and written in the slang[53] used by the drivers. For fun, I sent in a submission, which they published immediately; and I went to visit the editorial office, then located on the Palma side street. On the ground floor was a greasy spoon owned by the same fellow who owned the newspaper in the offices above, which was edited by a dark, chubby man who wrote almost all of the eight weekly pages. He signed the different sections with various pseudonyms; the truck terminals were covered by a thin individual, with bulging eyes, who signed his articles Mr. Crazy Man on the Skids.[54]

Within a few weeks, it was I who was writing and editing practically the entire newspaper. A sure instinct had associated me with the founders of a weekly that brought them numerous easy contacts among their specialized readers: drivers and bootlickers. Some of the best skins[55] of the time came to me lured by *El Chafirete*. The director preferred the little newsboys who sold the paper on the street; Mr. Crazy Man on the Skids (who died soon after in the Hospital de Jesús), the young subscription collectors; and I, the more solid drivers. I abused my own resistance and competitive ability to accommodate the most enormous dicks. And determined to conquer a kind of championship, I dared what everyone knew only his lover Nacho Moctezuma could tolerate: Agustín Fink's cock, whose diameter positively matched a can of salmon. Conscious of its gigantism, I cautiously introduced it while it was "asleep" and well coated with the lubricant we had before the meritorious advent of KY: *Vaseline*. But once inside, it opened like an umbrella, smashing up the walls of its narrow confinement. It opened a painful fissure in me that the unguents Suzuki relied on in such cases—a black zinc oxide pomade—didn't heal. I had to become a daily client of a Dr. Voiers, whose waiting room was full of plaintive victims of hemorrhoids and other rear-end deteriorations. He had me climb up on his examining table, opened my buttocks, and inserted a small roll of cotton moistened with burning ointments, which I was to keep in for the whole day.

I was still following this treatment when Pedro returned from South America. His disciples had sent him very bad reports about my person. I noticed this when, serious and mistrustful, he called me to his office. Beating about the bush, he went skirting around a confession—when it was I who burned to confess. He was more nervous than ever. He blinked his small, very black eyes, cleared his throat, moved his toes inside his shoes. Finally: "Would you do it with me?" And he drew near, as though he expected a kiss.

The scene was grotesque, but I measured the advantages of pleasing him: the jobs he had gotten me, the easy money, the agreeable work . . . And, after all, that swarthy fellow was no more ugly or unpleasant than that Heliodoro who one Sunday had persuaded me to visit him and received me in his pajamas. "Yes," I said, "if you wish . . ."

"But it is very bad," he replied, moving away, recovering himself, returning to his big rolltop desk. "It is a dirty act and unjustifiable. Certainly there can exist an attraction between two men, the impulse to kiss each other. In the university where I was teaching in the United States, a very handsome boy was drawn to me. We often conversed, as I am with you. And then one day: *I feel like kissing you*, he said. And I: *Go ahead*. And he kissed me here, on the cheek. But it's wrong. It shouldn't be."

Fortunately, someone entered to interrupt the scene. But to my disgrace, I didn't realize that as I was leaving, I expelled the cotton that, hours before, Dr. Voiers had inserted into my anus, and that it had fallen to the floor: evidence of the crime that must have infuriated the deceived Pedro, who took back, in the most combative, enraged enmity, all the favors that he had once bestowed on me.

Meanwhile, the effects of politics were felt in the court of the omnipotent Vasconcelos. From the University, to which he had appointed Pedro, he [Vasconcelos] leapt at the opportunity to found a Ministry of Education, taking Jaime Torres Bodet with him as head of the department of libraries. Thus began the long, firm, sure, aseptic career, during the many years of which he would twice return to Education to be its minister. Jaime surrounded himself with a small court of Mexican and Central American poets and journalists, who visited him every morning to shower him with praise.

At the University, whose satisfied rector was the philosopher Antonio Caso, content to have a close shave, climb into his Ford, and go for tea at the Lady Baltimore; the group that was addicted to Pablo Henríquez Ureña was adverse to the group around Jaime and Vasconcelos. Counted in the first were Vicente Lombardo Toledano, director of the Preparatoria, and Daniel Cosío Villegas, director of the University Extension, who, at Pedro's suggestion, had named me a "lecturer" (I had to take a streetcar, twice a week, all the way to the villages of San Gregorio Atlapulco and Tulyehualco to talk to the Indians about things they didn't understand. To keep myself from quitting the job, I "made" the streetcar driver, right away, then and there.) As though in reply to the [Ministry of] Education group's magazine *La Falange* (which published a long excerpt from my narrative *El Joven* [The Young Man], the University group brought out the single issue of its *Vida Mexicana* [Mexican Life].

The intractable argument between Vasconcelos and Henríquez Ureña and his group culminated in the downfall of the former, and the resignations of Caso and Pedro, who, before leaving, had violently stripped me of my jobs, after an inflamed scene in which he preached that, for my eventual salvation, I had to suffer ordeals and privations, *go shovel snow in New York*, to toughen me up. Then he proclaimed his upcoming wedding to Isabel Lombardo, Vicente's youngest and prettiest sister. I gave myself the negative pleasure of attending the ceremony in the San Cosme church. Julio Torri would later tell Montenegro the slanderous lie that during the ceremony I had opened my arms, gotten down on my knees, and implored all through the wedding: "Lord, protect him, Lord take care of him for me, whatever will he do with a woman?"

How well it all turned out: with the kind enthusiasm of the gringas who found me *Oh, so young, so cute, and yet so learned,*[56] I had acquired a certain right to keep the Summer School class in

Mexican literature. Its new director—having gone to Argentina on his honeymoon, Pedro Henríquez Ureña never returned—was, recently returned from Europe, that dark, severe Moisés Sáenz whom I had seen, one tumultuous afternoon, get thrown out of the Preparatoria. He conceded that I could teach the class, but treated me with marked reserve. Only much later, when we became friends, did he confide to me that before leaving, Pedro had made the express recommendation that he not give me employment.

Clarita returned from Europe. His natural, charming gaiety was now accentuated by the refinement that he had acquired there: cocaine. He kept the crystal dust in a little metal box covered with fake jewels, and taught me to appreciate the delight of that sudden, intensifying, pervasive sharpening of the mind as it fastened on the elements and details that go unnoticed in the clumsiness of one's normal state.

I hastened to share my discovery of this new taste with Xavier and Delfino. Having Uncle Miguel's prescription pad close at hand made it easy for me to steal a page on which I'd written: "Script: Hydrochloride of cocaine, 1 grm," adding a scribble for a signature. Any apothecary would fill the order: at 2.50 pesos for one gram of the purest cocaine. Although we began our doses[57] in some enclosed redoubt, hyperkinesia soon had us walking tirelessly, unceasingly through the streets; talking, drained of any petty need such as hunger or sleep. Sexual activity was relegated to a second plane. Pleasure came in that exalted nervousness, in that refined, elevated, magnificent synesthesia that brought every perception almost to the point of paroxysm, and that dissected the most unexpected and lucid metaphors when, under the influence of the drug, I elaborated poems that my insomnia—full of strident cardiac palpitations—polished in my mind.

Happy to have made us proselytes for "snow," Clara brought us to visit his new friends. We went one night to see Violeta, an old whore who had completely erased her North American origins and received at her small house the lovers of her daughter Irene and of a niece, Milagros, whose lover was Ernesto García Cabral,[58] famous among them for his big black dick. The actor Luis G. Barreiro[59] was Violeta's lover. When Violeta drank too many cognacs, which she alternated with cocaine, she would sink into melancholy silence. She would stare forlornly at the floor and after a long while sigh, "What shame, for a girl to fall in love with a male whore!" Because in that state, she believed she was in love with Clara.

Sinking deeper and deeper into his cocaine habit, Clara started to lose his mind. And one of his flights of madness consisted of falling in love with a *loca*, he who always preached the superstitious creed that one *loca* falling in love with another simply ruined himself. Carlos Luquín,[60] or Elena Luca, as Clara himself had christened him, was suddenly the object of his [Clara's] attentions, the support and authority that Clara craved. Knowing full well that Luquín would be going to the baths to have his bones rubbed, along with the other clients at the famed San Agustín (whole-body massage. One had to ask Chon for the personal steam treatment); or to visit Cushion Cunt, Clara would wait for him all night, leaning on the railing of the balcony of his new, gloomy apartment across from Plaza Río de Janeiro; shaking the little box until the provision of "snow" was all gone, and the sun was coming up, he would then inject himself with a sedative so he could collapse into bed—from which one day his powerful relatives would remove, and all but secretly bury the squalid body, which had been consumed alive.

As long as his Socratic tutelage lasted, Pedro Henríquez Ureña insisted that I do writing exercises to bring my prose into the realm of intelligibility. "It is necessary that you learn to write like Carlos González Peña," he would say with barely concealed sarcasm for the editor of [the newspaper] *El Universal*. And he made me earn extra money by sending my articles and editorials to *El Mundo*, the newspaper directed by Martín Luis Guzmán. In this way I learned how easy it was to get in the door of journalism. *El Universal Ilustrado* welcomed my contributions with disproportionately enthusiastic praise; so that even though they paid very little—ten pesos for an article of three manuscript pages—I was not entirely without income, until suddenly the annihilating hatred of the disappointed master deprived me of the assignments that had been showered upon me.

I was nearly twenty years old. My quitting law school had not been a major disappointment to my family. They knew that instead I was already working, like all my uncles, who had done so from a young age, with the exception of Manuel, an academic. That calmed them, or at least explained their indifference toward me. I could already contribute now and then some portion of the household expenses, pay for my own clothes, and do my best to avoid the torture of sitting at the family table only to brood on my sense of guilt before the bourgeois normality of my uncle Salvador, the haughty indifference of Manuel, the sorrowful slimness of Julia, and the pure matriarchy of my grandmother. I quickly dispatched breakfast and the midday meal, and accustomed them not to count on me for dinner.

At the Antonios' studio, I met Enrique Jiménez. He was giving a course on English literature at Advanced Studies and was friends with and of the same generation as characters like Antonio Caso[61] and Genaro Fernández MacGregor;[62] but he cultivated a more intimate friendship with Honorato Bolaños—Totó—who was Antonio Caso's second-in-command at Advanced Studies, being secretary or director of the faculty.

Enrique demonstrated an admiration for Totó with which he masked his own shyness in order to dare what Totó already had daringly acquired: an enormous clientele of cadets, firemen, and gendarmes with whom he organized individual orgies at his house on [Calle] Ernesto Pugibet, strategically close to the firemen's barracks and the always well-stocked Plaza de la Ciudadela. It is possible that if Enrique had asked Totó if he would cede him one or two of his many skins, the old fellow would have agreed to this easy liberation from the ones he was tired of. But Enrique, even knowing full well that he was only gathering up the leftovers, preferred to do his hunting as they entered or left *chez* Totó, from the car in which he cruised interminably through all the city's dark streets, only to keep passing Totó's door, trying to induce, by whether his lights were on or off, what the one whose audacity he envied must be doing; and finally invite one of Totó's late-arriving clients to climb into his car.

We discussed how neither of us had a "studio"; and at his suggestion, we decided to rent one together. He showed me a house—42 Calle Brasil—where they rented "offices." Very close to the schools: half a block from Medicine; and what for me was more important, very close to the Department of Transportation, then located at the Santo Domingo Customs House and always full of drivers getting or renewing their licenses.

On the top floor, which was vacant, there was a furnished room with a sink. I leased it: thirty pesos a month. Nothing more fit in it (and nothing more was needed) than a bed, a chair, a console table over which I hung a Saint Ignatius that I'd bought for ten pesos from Pepe Alcalde, and a folding screen that I had made to provide artful access to the bed, and to hide what would go on there. A small window ventilated the room and allowed one to look down on Calle de Brasil. We arranged a signal to indicate when the coast was clear and when the room was in use; a sash—leftover from the nationalist measles of the first "studio"—would be hung in the window as a warning not to climb all the steps of that enormous staircase.

And so we were in business: I brought in the willing drivers and bus conductors, and he brought to the room the cadets he used to pick off from *chez* Totó.

I invited Xavier, Delfino, and Montenegro to my new residence. Xavier had stopped being lovers with the Virgin, and learned to procure the passive little ragamuffins he liked. I began to be friends with Agustín Lazo, Antonio Adalid's nephew. Antonio had told me: "I have a very hypocritical 'niece.' I wish 'she'd' let 'her' hair down. I'm going to introduce you." And one night he invited a plain young introverted fellow, whose hair was plastered flat to his head, and who oozed culture and inhibition through his buttoned-up suit. He was painting, and current with literature and music. He insisted on talking about art and blushed at every joke of his boisterous uncle, who never stopped observing him and made me want to gain the nephew's reluctant trust.

With Xavier, on the other hand, Agustín immediately got on well. With no inhibitions, the two of them took the vacant room next to the one I had rented on the top floor. Agustín brought fine velvet pillows from his own house.

Shy Enrique must have found my many friends coming to our room, and the invasion of competitors on the other floors, uncomfortable or dangerous. On one of those floors, Javier Villada Saviñón kept his colorfully upholstered room; and Montenegro, then installed at San Pedro y San Pablo (where he established his studio outside the temple declared by Vasconcelos the "Hall of Free and Open Discussion," and painted a fresco), took another room in our building. All of which induced Enrique to leave, set up his headquarters elsewhere.

On the top floor, apart from the rooms rented by me and by Xavier and Agustín, was one occupied by a student from Veracruz, and the ones where María, the caretaker, and her family lived: her ancient mother, Jorgita; her brother Jorge and his daughter Carmen. All short and squat like identical dwarfs. After doing our rooms, María spent the morning leaning over the washboard, rubbing almost to shreds our cloth handkerchiefs, from which, years later, with the benediction of Kleenex, we would finally be free. And at night, she would carry halfway down the stairs a small mattress, on which she would doze, ready to open the door each time a lodger, at unexpected hours, started up the stairs accompanied by a quick shadow.

"This flower of fourteen petals"

Salvador Novo and the Sonnet

MARGUERITE FEITLOWITZ

SALVADOR NOVO, who wrote sonnets in every period of his creative life, was proud to be obsessed with what he called "this flower of fourteen petals." Playing on the gender values of his native Spanish, he said the *soneto* was the "gallant husband" of the *sonata* in a marriage of music and mind, sense and sensibility. "All the differences they have had throughout the centuries are conjugated in formal serenity," he wrote in the introduction to *Mil y un sonetos mexicanos* [A Thousand and One Mexican Sonnets), the anthology he edited in 1963, which embraced the period of the Spanish Conquest to the present.[1] Novo maintained that he could have included thousands more poems. (It is possible that no one at the time had read more Mexican sonnets than Salvador Novo.) His arrangement of poems demonstrated the perennial immediacy of the sonnet: rather than reify his choices chronologically, he grouped his selections from multiple centuries within broad rubrics: Love (of course), Epic, Funerary, Nature, Landscape, Environment, Mysticism and Religion, Humor, Self-Portrait, and Various (which brought together narrative and philosophical poems, sonnets with classical references and themes, poems on music and on poetry itself). Novo's population of poets within each rubric infuses the category itself with energy: Sor Juana in epic form along with Anonymous of 1640, and a number of poets commemorating students (Mateana Murguía de Aveleyra), peasants (Ignacio Ramírez), and children (Novo) mowed down by colonizers; Villaurrutia, Nandino, and Pellicer, with the eighteenth-century Diego José Plancarte; "A Sonnet to the Moon," "Ixtapalapa," "Anáhuac," "To the Ixmiquilpan River," together with urban scenes from the likes of Paz, Reyes, and Ramos. Most of the poets appear in multiple guises: Sor Juana (almost everywhere, including Humor); Villaurrutia in Love as well as Religion and Mysticism; Alfonso Reyes in Love and Humor and Funerary. Especially moving are the funerary sonnets dedicated to fellow poets (Paz on Jorge Cuesta, for example). Novo included some of his own poems in the Love, Epic, and Mysticism and Religion sections, but the largest selection of his sonnets appears in Various; these eight poems were written between 1955 and 1960 and are identified by year.

Their major preoccupation is with the dreads, regrets, and ravages exacted by the passing years; "To Xavier Villaurrutia," however, bears no date, for this was an eternal friendship, beyond the constraints of time.

The constraints of the sonnet, however, were delicious and liberating for Novo. He made extensive use, in his own work, of this elegant form: here, it sings the praises of fallen child soldiers; here, it serenades the broken heart; here again, it worships the beloved; now it worships God; here, it praises the *patria*; here, it decries all forms of public power. Novo infuses his sonnets with the characteristics of other literary genres: he sets the scene; weaves a plot; establishes a palpable identity for both the speaker and the one to whom the lines are addressed; he creates and manipulates our expectations; he draws us in, often, ultimately, to fence us out. His sonnets combine the epistolary and dramatic monologue; elegy (for love, for youth, for beauty) with satire; fondness with fear and loathing (of self and others). Novo's sonnets are by turns hilarious, solemn, and sarcastic (swaggering Diego Rivera, shot full of darts!); they are often about sex—young and radiant, yearning and old, dirty and down.

No matter where the Novo sonnet goes, it is always impeccably turned out. His favored structure is composed of two quatrains followed by two tercets, in a rhyme scheme of abba, abba, cdc, dcd. Sudden shifts in tone are lubricated by regular rhymes. His lines, usually of twelve or thirteen syllables, are consistent without feeling rigid. He turns the form's predictability to surprising, and very shrewd, rhetorical advantage. (The sonnet is, after all, by definition an *argument*.) In Novo's Spanish, the pattern of end rhymes makes us anticipate certain phonemes; however, the actual word that completes the rhyme is not infrequently shocking—flippant, slangy, scatological. Without violating the smoothness of the sonnet, Novo nonetheless "yanks" our head around, scrambles whatever assumptions we might harbor about the form. Even as he vaunts his technical mastery, Novo undermines our trust in forms per se (including norms of address and association, of behavior and belief, of display and disguise). Whatever the subject, the music flows. The rhymes take us in hand, leading us down the garden path or into brambles of disappointed love; alleyways and truck stops; dark hollows of the body, mind, and spirit.

In the erotic sonnets gathered here, Novo plays a number of roles, and he plays them to the hilt: he is by turns wheedling and aggressive, seductive and evasive, playfully pathetic and grinningly cruel (not least to himself). His final tercets tend to be abrupt, leaving us suddenly alone. Yet many of his sonnets are poignant, even nakedly soulful, as is the powerful Sonnet XVII.

The sonnets in this volume come from two Novo collections, published in Mexico by Guillermo Rousset Banda: *Dieciocho sonetos* [Eighteen Sonnets, 1954] and the *Poesía Completa* [Complete Poetry, 1955]. The nineteenth sonnet, composed later, was originally published in a posthumous anthology of Novo's poems. The present grouping of sonnets was included as an appendix to the 1996 publication in Mexico of *Estatua de sal*.

Novo, the provocateur, was a stickler for rules (and wrote scathingly of poets who "cheated" in their sonnets, fudging their syllables, furring their rhymes). My own first rule was, "Do No Harm." Readers of Spanish will note that I have taken some liberties, but only as part of my effort to stay true to the original. While I retained Novo's stanzas, and kept the line length as consistent as felt right, I chose not to reproduce his exact rhyme scheme. In English, rhymes that in Spanish seem natural and fluid often sound forced. But rhyme is essential to these erotic sonnets; and so I opted for rhymes that are irregular, but which I hope capture the elegance and surprise of the originals.

Sonnets

SALVADOR NOVO

I

Escribir porque sí, por ver si acaso
se hace un soneto más que nada valga;
para matar el tiempo, y porque salga
una obligada consonante al paso.

Porque yo fui escritor, y éste es el caso
que era tan flaco como perra galga;
crecióme la papada como nalga,
vasto de carne y de talento escaso.

¡Qué le vamos a hacer! Ganar dinero
y que la gente nunca se entrometa
en ver si se lo cedes a tu cuero.

Un escritor genial, un gran poeta . . .
Desde los tiempos del señor Madero,
es tanto como hacerse la puñeta.

I

Why not write just to see if perhaps
there comes a sonnet worth more than a dime;
Why not write just to kill time, to cross paths
along the way with an obligatory rhyme.

For I was a writer, and it can't be denied
I was lean as a greyhound bitch;
my jowls have grown fat as my buttocks,
my flesh is fat, my talent bollocks.

What can we do! We must get rich
others should mind their own business
why shouldn't we sell our own hides.

A writer of brilliance, a poet who merits ovation,
from the times of Mister Madero
the very idea is masturbation.

II

Si yo tuviera tiempo, escribiría
mis memorias en libros minuciosos;
retratos de políticos famosos,
gente encumbrada, sabia y de valía.

¡Un Proust que vive en México! Y haría
por sus hojas pasar los deliciosos
y prohibidos idilios silenciosos
de un chofer, de un ladrón, de un policía.

Pero no puede ser, porque juiciosa-
mente pasa la doble vida mía
en su sitio poniendo cada cosa.

Que los sabios disponen de mi día,
y me aguarda en la noche clamorosa
la renovada sed de un policía.

II

If I had time, I would write
my memoirs: volumes of minutiae,
portraits of enlightened men,
wise and valiant politicians.

A Proust who lives in Mexico! In these
pages I would paint the wordless idylls—
delicious and forbidden—
of a chauffeur, a robber, a policeman.

It cannot be, so cautious-
ly does my double life define
a single place for every single item.

Let upright men rule my days,
and let me hope in the clamorous night
for the renewing thirst of a policeman.

III

Este fácil soneto cotidiano
que mis insomnios nutre y desvanece,
sin objeto ni dádiva se ofrece
al nocturno sopor del sueño vano.

¡Inanimado lápiz que en mi mano
mis odios graba o mis ensueños mece!
En tus concisas líneas aparece
la vida fácil, el camino llano.

Extinguiré la luz. Y amanecida,
el diamante de ayer será al leerte
una hoguera en cenizas consumida.

Y he de concluir, soneto, y contenerte
como destila el jugo de la vida
la perfección serena de la muerte.

III

This facile quotidian sonnet,
feeding, fading, on the edges of my sleep,
is offered unbidden and without bounty
to the nocturnal torpor of vain dreaming.

Inanimate pencil which in my hand
records my hates, and rocks my dreams!
In your narrow lines appear
this life that is facile, this road that is flat.

I will extinguish the light. At dawn
the diamond of yesterday will be
to read you—a bonfire hallowed in ash.

My sonnet, I must conclude, strain you
as the juice of life distills
the serene perfection of death.

IV

Ya no parece bien, a mis abriles,
pensar en el amor. Fuera locura
llorar, sentir, querer—¡ay!—con la pura
ilusión de los años juveniles.

No sueño más en lunas ni pensiles
ni de un ósculo pido la dulzura
al fuego que en mis sienes se apresura
—con patriótico ardor—en los desfiles.

La ley de la demanda y de la oferta
que me ha enseñado su sabiduría
lleva el fácil amor hasta mi puerta.

Y sin embargo, a veces, todavía
sobre el crespón de mi esperanza muerta
vierte su llanto la melancolía.

IV

It's not good now, in my months of May
to think of love. Away madness
crying, feeling, wanting—away!—with youth
and its years of pure illusion.

I no longer dream of the moon or a garden glade
nor ask for the burning sweetness of a kiss
so like the pulsing—patriotic—ardor
aroused by soldiers on parade.

The law of demand and supply
that taught me the wherefores and why
delivers love that's easy to buy.

And yet, there are times, when
the dark veils of hope that died
are rent with melancholy weeping.

V

Mi vida sigue igual, amiga rara:
Despierto hecho una birria, voy al baño
y con productos Rubinstein restaño
la perdida frescura de mi cara.

Me marcho a trabajar. ¡Si trabajara!
El boletín del mes, año tras año . . .
Luego voy a comer con el extraño
ministro que la suerte me depara.

Doy a veces mi clase consabida;
a mi oficina soñoliento llego;
mi labor oficial quedó cumplida.

Y a las dulzuras del hogar me entrego
cuando ya mi clientela conocida
me almidonó las tripas en San Diego.

V

My life goes on as usual, why dear friend would you ask:
awake and a horror, I head for the bath
and with Helena Rubinstein lotions and creams
staunch the wrinkles, mend the seams.

I go to work. But is it *work*?
the monthly bulletin, year after year . . .
then lunch with the oddball
Minister fate has assigned me here.

Sometimes I give my usual class;
sleepily arrive at my office;
there, I've completed my official tasks.

Now it's home sweet home and fare you well;
my guts are bored
by my usual clientele.

VI

Yo te aguardé esta noche con el ansia
de mirarte llegar, y de que luego
escucharas impávido mi ruego
y me dieras tu fuerza y tu fragancia.

Pero quisiste darte la elegancia
de no venir, de desdeñar mi fuego,
sin saber que recibo por entrego
leche de muchos toros en mi estancia.

Yo pensaba quererte en exclusiva;
gemir y sollozar bajo tu fuete,
brindarte mis pasiones rediviva.

Y a casa regresé—con tu billete—,
luego que una salubre lavativa
a los hijos ahogó de otro cadete.

VI

I watched for you tonight, eager
to see you arrive, knowing that later
you would listen, impassive, to your beggar
and then give in—ravishing, strong, and fragrant.

But no, you opted for the elegant
disdain of not coming. Ignorant
that on my estates are many bulls
whose milk I entirely own.

I thought that I would love you, and you alone;
that beneath your whip, I would sob and moan
and honor you with new-fired passion.

But home I came—with your theater stub—
after salubrious attentions
to an inhibited cub.

VII

¿Por qué no me has escrito en tantos días
en que angustiado y pálido me espero
a que llegue el simpático cartero
espiando tras las blancas celosías?

Yo pensé que más veces mentirías
tu amor lejano, dulce y plañidero;
que el engaño siguiera lisonjero
que iniciaron tus cartas y las mías.

¿Qué te cuesta decirme que me adoras?
¿Qué me cuesta creerlo y consolarme
lejos de ti, mi bien, si me enamoras?

¿Qué te cuesta en epístola besarme?
Yo pienso en ti por indelebles horas
—y hace en ellas tus veces un gendarme.

VII

Why after so many days have you not written
while I, pale and tormented, keep waiting,
watching behind white blinds
for the merciful arrival of a letter?

I thought it far more likely that you would lie
in the tender reams of a lover's laments,
that praise would precede deception
in your letters and mine.

What would it cost you to say you adore me?
What would it cost me to believe the story,
now we are parted, that you love me?

What would it cost you to kiss me in a letter?
The hours I think of you are indelible
and the charms of my policeman untellable.

VIII

Yo te escribiera a diario, dueño mío:
fatigara tus ojos con mi anhelo;
diera al papel las tintas de mi duelo
y al sol la angustia de mi lecho frío.

Pero, ¿cómo plasmar mi desvarío
con palabras escritas en el hielo
deste común hablar, luz de mi cielo,
deste lenguaje pródigo y vacío?

¿Cómo mi muda voz expresaría
todo el amor, en lágrimas deshecho
que riega en aguardarte mi agonía?

Grite tu corazón, con el estrecho
mensaje de su voz, la vida mía
en la dorada cárcel de tu pecho.

VIII

I could write you every day, my darling lord,
wear your eyes out with my longing
dim the page with signs of my sorrow
and the sun with the anguish of my bed.

But how, light of my heaven,
give form to my delirium
in the ice of this common idiom
with words that are prodigal, and hollow?

How, with muted voice, express
this love undone by weeping,
when all it begs to offer is distress?

If your heart would only
speak its meaning: my life
in the golden prison of your breast.

IX

Escribirte otra vez, ir al Correo;
tocar mi lengua sus orillas frías;
llevar la cuenta exacta de los días
que hace que se efectuó nuestro himeneo.

Pensar que hace ya mucho que no veo
tus ojos claros y tus manos mías;
aguardar tu respuesta en las vacías
horas en que en pensarte me recreo.

Robar al sueño la ilusión de verte
y a la vigilia el dulce de soñarte
con temor y esperanza de perderte.

No hallar tu imagen en ninguna parte;
eso es amor, mi bien, y de esta suerte,
vivo y muero tan sólo en aguardarte.

IX

Writing once again to you, going to the Post;
touching my tongue to its frigid coast;
counting precisely the number of days
that have elapsed since our hymeneal.

Thinking how long it's been since I've
seen your blue eyes, your hands that are mine;
these empty hours of awaiting you,
of thinking you, revivify my soul for you.

Robbing the dream of the illusion of seeing you
and the vigil of the sweetness of dreaming you
in the fear and expectation of losing you.

Never finding but always looking for you;
that is love, my treasure, what can I do,
I shall live and I shall die awaiting you.

X

Pienso, mi amor, en ti todas las horas
del insomnio tenaz en que me abraso;
quiero tus ojos, busco tu regazo
y escucho tus palabras seductoras.

Digo tu nombre en sílabas sonoras,
oigo el marcial acento de tu paso,
te abro mi pecho—y el falaz abrazo
humedece en mis ojos las auroras.

Está mi lecho lánguido y sombrío
porque me faltas tú, sol de mi antojo,
ángel por cuyo beso desvarío.

Miro la vida con mortal enojo;
y todo esto me pasa, dueño mío,
porque hace una semana que no cojo.

X

I think, in these hours, of you, my love,
burning as I do in merciless insomnia;
wanting your eyes, seeking the curve of your hip,
I feel the promises impressed by your lips.

I repeat the ringing syllables of your name,
hear the martial accent of your step;
I open my chest, I bare my heart—this
weepy embrace is but lying art.

My bed is languid and lugubrious,
for you, sun of my craving, angel of kisses,
are gone, and I am alone and delirious.

I look at life with mortal rue;
all this, my lord, is due to you,
for it's a week since I have screwed.

XI

¿Qué hago en tu ausencia? Tu retrato miro;
él me consuela lo mejor que puedo;
si me caliento, me introduzco el dedo
en efigie del plátano a que aspiro.

Ya sé bien que divago y que deliro,
y sé que recordándote me enredo
al grado de tomar un simple pedo
por un hondo y nostálgico suspiro.

Pero en esta distancia que te aleja,
dueño de mi pasión, paso mi rato,
o por mejor decir, me hago pendeja,

ora con suspirar, ora con pedo,
premiando la ilusión de tu retrato
y los nuevos oficios de mi dedo.

XI

What do I do in your absence? I stare at your picture
trying as best I can for consolation;
when I get hot, I introduce a finger
in effigy of the plantain I pine for.

I know that I rave and wander
in remembering you,
confuse the simple urge to fart
with a deep and yearning exhalation.

Distant lord of my passion,
without you here, I while away my time,
or better said, keep hanging on.

Now with a sigh, now with a fart
praising the illusions of the painter's art
and the newfound talents of my finger.

SALVADOR NOVO

XII

Leoncio ayer, Carlos hoy—¿a quién mañana
dedicará mi amor su pensamiento?
¿Quién con su ausencia me dará el tormento
de esta esperanza dulce, pero vana?

Salvaje en uno, me embriagó la sana
y cálida caricia de su aliento.
Amo en el otro, príncipe de cuento,
la mirada magnífica y lejana.

Aceite de mi lámpara, que ensartas
en rosarios de tiempo duradero
ilusión y fragancia de sus cartas.

No te daré mi amor, casual viajero,
pero mi lecho es amplio; y cuando partas,
te llevarás un poco de dinero.

XII

Leon yesterday, Carlos today—toward whom
will my cupid mind be drawn tomorrow?
Whose absence will come as a gift of sorrow,
the sweetness of hope that is hollow?

With one I could forever laze
in the warm caress of his breath;
But the fairy-tale prince commands my love
with the splendor of his distant gaze.

Light of my life, you link my days of
waiting for the perfumed letters you never send
as though they were beads in a rosary without end.

Be not deceived, I know you're passing through,
my bed, however, is big enough for two; but, honey,
you must take a little money when you leave.

XIII

¡Ay, qué castillos fabriqué en el viento
cuando tu voz acarició mi oído
y al cielo que me tengo prometido
mi esperanza asomé por un momento!

¡Qué rápido viajó mi pensamiento!
¡Cómo en tus brazos me soñé, transido
del goce amargo de usurpar un nido,
morder tus labios y beber tu aliento!

¡Cómo soñé fundir en las miradas
de tus ojos de fuego, la alegría
deste hielo que vuelves llamaradas!

(Pero al llegar el anhelado día,
como cuadra a personas educadas,
dormimos—tú en tu cama, y yo en la mía.)

XIII

Oh, the palaces I built in the breeze
as your voice caressed the air
and my hopes, taking the dare,
soared to high heaven!

How my thoughts raced!
How I dreamed of lying in your embrace,
the bitter pleasure of usurping a nest,
of biting your lips and drinking your breath!

How I dreamed of melting in the fire
of your eyes, of how my joyful heart
would rhapsodize!

(But as befits well-mannered humankind
when the day arrived for which we pined,
we slept—you in your bed, I in mine.)

SALVADOR NOVO

XIV

Si pudieras quedarte, dueño mío;
si yo pudiera compartir tu lecho;
sentir tu corazón junto a mi pecho
vibrar en jubiloso desvarío;

pasar toda una noche, dueño mío,
entre tu abrazo férvido y estrecho;
entregarte la vida, y satisfecho,
la vida reanudar con nuevo brío.

Pero es fuerza partir. Un lecho frío
me depara el silencio de su abrigo,
tan correcto—tan amplio—y tan vacío.

¡Mañana nos veremos! Y me digo,
"Que a dormir a tu lado, dueño mío,
siempre será mejor soñar contigo."

XIV

If only you could stay, my lord;
if only I could share your bed,
feel your heart against my breast
quiver like a bride's.

If only I could spend all night, my lord,
wrapped tight in your embrace;
surrender my life, and satisfied,
awake with you, revivified.

But you must go. My cold bed
is left holding your coat,
so proper—so pillowy—and cast away.

Until tomorrow! But to myself I say,
"My lord, to sleep through the night with you
would be far better than to dream of you."

XV

Me dije: "Ya por fin la vida mía
el objeto encontró de su ternura;
es él quien llenará con su dulzura
para todos los siglos mi alegría".

Pero un año pasó desde aquel día;
monótona tornóse mi ventura,
y vi junto a su carne prematura
huerto en sazón que mieles ofrecía.

Déjame en mi camino. Por fortuna
ni el Código Civil ha de obligarte
ni tuvimos familia inoportuna.

El tiempo ha de ayudarme a subsanarte.
Nada en mí te recuerda—salvo una
leve amplitud mayor—en cierta parte.

XV

I said to myself: "This heart of mine
has found the object for its fondness;
he, with whose eternal sweetness,
I shall live entwined."

But since that day a year has come and gone:
my affair, turned dull, keeps going on;
in the garden of his tender flesh
I see offerings no longer fresh.

So go. According to the Civil Code,
nothing more is owed; between us, no
accidental family was ever sowed.

Time must help me pardon you.
With thoughts of you—these don't come often—
A certain cleft can't help but soften.

XVI

Ya se acerca el invierno, dueño mío;
estas noches solemnes y felices,
se ponen coloradas las narices
y se parten las manos con el frío.

Ven a llenar mi corazón vacío
harto de sinsabores y deslices
en tanto que preparo las perdices,
que pongo la sartén—y que las frío.

Deja tu mano encima de la mía;
dígame tu mirada milagrosa
si es verdad que te gusto—todavía.

Y hazme después la consabida cosa
mientras un Santa Claus de utilería
cava un invierno más en nuestra fosa.

XVI

Winter is upon us, darling lord;
these glad and solemn nights
bite our noses, split the skin
between our fingers.

Come fill my hungry heart;
I offer you a feast:
partridges and pears
and every kind of sweet.

Lay your hand on mine;
if you should want me still,
let your eyes pronounce the miracle.

Come be my Christmas wish made true,
though I know my winter, with you
or without you, will be dark and chill.

XVII

Tus manos fuertes, grandes, que me daban
la vida en sus caricias, y la muerte;
mis manos, que quisieron retenerte;
tus manos, que mi pecho desgarraban.

Tus manos, que en la sangre se pintaban
del corazón que palpitó por verte;
mis manos, sacudidas de su inerte
vacío si a las tuyas se enlazaban.

El milagro ocurrió. No fueron vanos
a los ojos de Dios mis hondos ruegos
ni mis suspiros sordos y lejanos.

Y volvieron a ver mis ojos ciegos
tintas en sangre tus soñadas manos
(pero sangre de reses—y borregos).

XVII

Your strong hands, caressing me
back to life, and unto death;
my hands, wanting to possess you;
your hands, ripping through my chest.

Your hands, soaked in the blood
of the heart that beat only to see you;
my hands, interlaced with your hands,
shaking in the void.

The miracle happened. In God's eyes
my deep prayers and distant
desperate sighs were not in vain.

My blind eyes had a vision:
painted in blood your dreamed-of hands
(but the blood of beasts—and lambs).

XVIII

Nos volvemos a ver. Año tras año
soñé con encontrarte en mi camino.
¡Sol de mis ojos, luz de mi destino!
¿No quisieras, mi bien, tomar un baño?

Nos encontramos uno al otro extraño:
Gordo tú, flaco yo—¡mundo mezquino!
Y me complace ver—¡oh, desatino!—
que hay cosas que no cambian de tamaño.

Te quiero como antaño te quería:
con pasión, con dolor, con amargura,
cual si este siglo hubiese sido un día.

Quiero corresponder a tu ternura:
Levanta tu barriga, vida mía,
que me voy a quitar—la dentadura.

XVIII

We meet again. Year after year
I dreamed of seeing you on my path.
Sunlit apparition, destiny shining clear!
But mightn't you like, my love, to take a bath?

We find each other very strange:
I slim, you fat; does the universe offer only *that*?
But I'm pleased to see—unless my sight be dim—
the size of some things doesn't change.

I love you now as I loved you then:
with passion, pain, and signs of decay
as though this century were but a day.

I want, like you, to be tender:
Sweetheart, suck in your paunch,
I need to remove—my denture.

XIX

Dura visión aflige a los longevos
—cáscara inútil en desierto nido—:
ver que se apaga en ellos la libido
—urgencia y potestad de los mancebos.

Ambos endocrinaran como nuevos
—fabricantes del jugo apetecido—
si el derecho no hubiera desistido
(hablo—¡triste experiencia!—de mis huevos).

Dura ley: pero ley que nos caduca,
todo—decreta—por servir se extingue:
ayer si penetró, sólo hoy machuca.

Puesto que ya no hay potro que respingue,
al consuelo falaz de una peluca
mi juventud se atenga—y yo me chingue.

XIX

Tough sight for the long-of-life
—useless shell in an empty nest—
seeing old libido go to its rest
—youth gets all the power and zest.

My two endocrinate[1] as though they were new
—producing that lovely nectar—
as though the law showed mercy once and for all
(I'm talking—sad to say!—of my balls).

Tough law: but the law causes us all
to expire; we are made in order to degenerate:
I used to be the man; now I'm barely a Kate.

Given that no colt would come hither
for the lying consolation of a wig,
my youth is fucked, I've only myself to frig.

Notes

INTRODUCTION

1. Monsiváis writes "gay"—without italics or quotation marks—in his original Spanish.
2. Jorge Cuesta (1903–1942) was a Mexican poet.
3. Carballo's *Diecinueve protagonistas de la literatura mexicana del siglo XX* was published in 1965, in Mexico City, by Empresas Editoriales. There seems to be no published English translation. Carballo, a prolific literary critic, was born in 1929.
4. Rafael Giménez Siles (1900–1991) was a Spanish publisher and cultural figure extremely active during the Second Republic. He organized the first Madrid Book Fair in 1933; established traveling libraries; and founded Nuestro Pueblo, which published Ramón del Valle-Inclán and Miguel Hernández among others, as well as the Biblioteca Popular de Cultura series. In 1939, he went into exile in Mexico (he took Mexican citizenship the following year); he is probably best known for having founded EDIAPSA (Ibero-American Publications Publishing and Distribution Co.), the Librerías Cristal bookstore chain.
5. Anastasio Bustamante (1780–1853), general and politician, was a three-term president of Mexico: 1830–1832, 1837–1839, and 1839–1841.
6. In the Spanish original.
7. The *porfiriato* refers to the long period (1876–1910) during which the conservative Porfirio Díaz was president of Mexico.
8. A zarzuela is a Spanish theater genre consisting of scenes that are alternately spoken and sung. They range from great librettos by the likes of Pedro Calderón de la Barca to light, frivolous operetta-type pieces, such as *Enseñanza libre* (whose title, "Free Instruction," is sexually mischievous). Spaniards Guillermo Perrín (1857–1923) and Miguel de Palacios (1863?–1920) were a prolific team whose literary gifts might have been dubious but earned them a fortune. The music for *Enseñanza libre* was written by Gerónimo Giménez (1854–1923), a Spanish composer admired for his technical skills.

9. Published in 1985 by UNAM; no English edition exists.
10. Emilio Portes Gil (1890–1978), president of the Republic, 1928–1930.
11. This male homosexual called himself "Pola Negri" after the legendary femme fatale and tragedienne of silent and talking films. Pola Negri was the stage name of the Polish-born Barbara Apolonia Chalupiec (1897–1987), who worked with Max Reinhardt and Ernst Lubitsch, among many others. She became a glamorous Hollywood star and was also a singer, ballerina, and writer.
12. Italics in original: "la *enfermedad nueva*."
13. Manuel Maples Arce (1898–1981), poet, lawyer, diplomat, was the founder of a movement he called *estridentismo*, or Stridentism, whose aesthetics mixed experimentation with thundering Bolshevist loyalties.
14. Antonio Ruiz (1892–1964), called "el Corzo" (the Roe Deer), on account of his short physical stature and his extraordinary resemblance to the famous Spanish bullfighter Manuel Corzo. He was a painter and a set designer for theater and in Hollywood. In 1943, he became head of the National School for Painting, Sculpture, and Prints (known as "La Esmeralda"), turning it into the official art school of the Ministry of Education.
15. The mostly Spanish-owned tobacco plantations in this region of the Yucatán were notoriously brutal, depending on slave labor, and supported by police, private guards, and bounty hunters to find runaways.
16. Julio Jiménez Rueda (1896–1960), lawyer, writer, playwright, diplomat, was the director of the Faculty of Philosophy and Literature at UNAM and taught Spanish literature there for many years.
17. Azuela's classic *Los de abajo* was first published in 1916. There is a new translation: *The Underdogs: A Novel of the Mexican Revolution*, translated by Sergio Waisman, with an essay by Carlos Fuentes (Penguin Classics, 2008).
18. Monsiváis writes "el *Come-out*" in his original.
19. Elías Nandino (1900–1993) was a physician and surgeon, as well as a notable poet, editor, and literary figure. The National Young Poets' Prize is named in his honor. The first collection of Nandino's poetry published in English appeared in 2010 from McFarland, a bilingual volume selected and translated by Don Cellini.
20. Monsiváis writes "*camp*" in his original.
21. This quote is taken from the paperback (New York: Ballantine Books, 1999), where it appears on p. 15.
22. Works by André Gide: *Corydon* (1924), available in Richard Howard's translation (University of Illinois Press, 2001); and *If It Die* (*Si le grain ne meure*), translated by Dorothy Bussy, Vintage reissue, 2001. *If It Die*, drafted between 1919 and 1924, is an autobiographical work.
23. My hunt for the origins of this quote was greatly helped by Joe Tucker, Reference Librarian, Bennington College, and by the International Shaw Society,

in particular Crista Zorn, who provided the following bibliographical details: The lines come at the end of a three-column article, "Oskar Wilde," by Bernard Shaw, that appeared in *Die Neue Freie Presse*, April 23, 1905, p. 38. The German text reads:

"Denn unsere heutigen Moralbegriffe sind ein ekelhafter, und wie Wilde gesagt haben würde, ein 'gemeiner' Irrtum. Sie sind nicht einmal sittlich. Und Wildes Anspruch auf Größe liegt in der Tatsache, daß unsere Sittlichkeit ihn nicht täuschen konnte und daß die Moralisten vergeblich seinen Geist zu brechen oder ihn zu schänden versucht haben.

"Er hat an seiner Pose bis ans Ende festgehalten, weil es eine ehrliche Pose war. Deshalb ist sie der englischen Sittlichkeit so unaussprechlich widerwärtig gewesen, denn diese ist auch eine Pose, aber ohne die Entschuldigung der Ehrlichkeit für sich zu haben."

24. Cernuda wrote "Si el hombre pudiera decir" in 1931.
25. Eliot Weinberger's fine English translation is found in *Nostalgia for Death & Hieroglyphs of Desire* (translated by Esther Allen), published in one volume by Copper Canyon Press in 1993.
26. Italicized in the Spanish original.
27. Written as "del amor *otro*" in the original Spanish.
28. It is "lujuria diferente" in the original.
29. One who has completed the undergraduate university degree, or *licencia*.

PILLAR OF SALT

1. Novo is referring to Juan de Dios Peza (1852–1910), scion of a prominent conservative family, whose numerous public positions included stints as ambassador to Spain and terms in Congress. Both a nationalist and a Hispanophile, Dios Peza founded the first society for Mexican authors and wrote poetry that was often ringingly patriotic. *Cantos del Hogar*—perhaps his most famous work—is based on his own experience of having been abandoned by his wife. His use of prosaic, everyday language is considered an important step past the old-fashioned romanticism that then characterized Mexican poetry.
2. Francisco I. Madero (1873–1913) headed the movement that brought down Porfirio Díaz. He was president of the Republic from 1911 until 1913, when he was overthrown and assassinated.
3. In Spanish, *coche* is a word for "car."
4. Troops and/or supporters of Pancho Villa (1878–1923). Essentially the caudillo of the state of Chihuahua, Villa was the commander of the Division of the North in the Mexican Revolution and at the height of his power between 1910 and 1920. Francisco ("Pancho") Villa was his pseudonym; he was born José Doroteo Arango Arámbula.

5. "La Adelita," a famous folksong of the Mexican Revolution, is about a woman who followed her lover into battle, not only nursing wounded soldiers and cooking meals at military encampments, but also taking up arms and proving herself valiant and brave. She was an archetypal figure of the time.
6. Italicized English word in Novo's original.
7. *Gachupín* (sing., also *gachupo*; pl., *gachupines*), a variation of *cachupín*, meaning a Spaniard who settled in Mexico.
8. *Popotillo*, a diminutive of *popote*, "thin straw."
9. *Espejo* was published in 1933.
10. Narciso Campillo y Correa (1835–1900) was a Spanish poet; rhetorician; writer of historical romances, short stories, and manuals on perception.
11. *L'homme qui rit*, by Victor Hugo, published in 1869.
12. Italicized English word in Novo's original.
13. The title translates as "Lots of Mustard" and alludes to a girl's "spicy" charms.
14. Venustiano Carranza de la Garza (1859–1920) was a leader of the Mexican Revolution and president of Mexico from 1917 to 1920. Army generals assassinated him because of his insistence that his successor be a civilian.
15. Justo Sierra Méndez (1848–1912) was a writer, historian, journalist, and poet who was involved with the founding of the National University of Mexico, now UNAM, National Autonomous University of Mexico.
16. José Natividad Macías (1857–1948) was a national representative in the last congress of the Porfirio Díaz presidency. In 1917, he was named rector of the National University, where he emphasized the development of scientific research laboratories.
17. José Vasconcelos (1882–1959) was named rector of the National University in 1920 and created the Ministry of Public Education in 1921. He is especially remembered for his support of muralists Diego Rivera and David Alfaro Siqueiros. He was named director of the Mexican National Library in 1940; and of the Institute for Hispanic Culture in 1948.
18. It appears that Novo is referring to Stephen de Bourret, the fourteenth-century bishop of Paris who, in 1324, supported Thomas Aquinas's belief that the soul is immortal.
19. Felipe Trigo (1864–1916), Spanish novelist who wrote erotic as well as realist books (*Las ingenuas*, *La sed de amar*, for example); Eduardo Zamacois (1876–1917), a Spaniard who also wrote erotic (*El seductor*), as well as realist novels (such as *Las raíces* [Roots]); Eduardo Marquina (1879–1946), Spanish poet and playwright (*En Flandes se ha puesto el sol* [The Sun Has Set Over Flanders], *Las hijas del Cid* [Daughters of El Cid], *Doña María la Brava* [Valiant Doña María]; Rubén Darío (1867–1916), the great Nicaraguan poet who, immersed in the Spanish Golden Age, influenced the development of twentieth-century lyric and political poetry; Emilio Carrere (1881–1947), bohemian Spanish journalist and poet.

20. Luis Coloma (1851–1914), Spanish Jesuit and writer who satirized the petty ways of the upper classes; and Juan Valera y Alcalá (1824–1905), Spanish diplomat, novelist, short-story writer, and essayist distinguished for his fine traditional style and elegant modes of thought.
21. The words *lobby* and, in the following paragraph, *cow-boy* and *close-ups* are italicized and in English in Novo's original.
22. Italicized English word in Novo's original.
23. *Melmoth the Wanderer* (1820), by Charles Robert Maturin, Oscar Wilde's maternal great uncle, concerns a scholar who sells his soul to the devil for an additional 150 years of life. The story, though set in the present, moves backward in time; and Melmoth is quite squalid.
24. As it appears in Novo's Spanish text.
25. Hermann Sudermann (1857–1928) was a German author of naturalist plays and novels.
26. Based on the novel by the great Benito Pérez Galdós (1843–1920), *Marianela,* a psychological work, centers on a young woman—an orphan—so small and innocent she looks like a child.
27. *La cena de las burlas* is a verse drama in four acts by Miguel Alessio Robles (1884–1951), a Mexican writer and political figure aligned with Venustiano Carranza.
28. Mexican mezzo-soprano (1887–1968).
29. A light meal, usually taken in the late afternoon or evening.
30. Carlos Meneses (d. 1929) was the first conductor of a Mexican symphony orchestra.
31. The nickname "Pedo Embotellado" can also be translated as "Bottled Fart," but since Novo refers to this person's "ridiculous stature," I chose "Cream Puff in a Corset." The Spanish double entendre is lost, but the visual cue is immediate, and some of these men did regularly wear corsets.
32. The word *amigas* (girlfriends) appears in Novo's Spanish text.
33. Novo italicizes *putear*.
34. Novo wrote *se salaba* in the original.
35. Novo uses the masculine pronoun (*él mismo*) in reference to Clara/Clara Vidal (Ricardo Alessio Robles), so I have done the same.
36. Edward Bradford Titchener (1867–1927), a British psychologist educated at Oxford and in Leipzig, was credited with founding structuralism (the study of the structure of the mind). He created, at Cornell University, the largest psychology department then in existence; under his tutelage, Margaret Floy Washburn became the first woman to receive a Ph.D. in psychology.
37. Julio Ruelas (1870–1907), Mexican painter and illustrator.
38. Adolfo de la Huerta (1881–1955) was interim president for the first six months of 1920.
39. Title given to the high priestess of the Temple of Apollo at Delphi; also known as the Oracle of Delphi.

40. "El Venadito" is a play on words, encompassing both "little faun" and "little whore."
41. The rose-colored stone used in pre-Columbian and traditional Mexican construction.
42. *Tepalcate* refers to earthen bowls and utensils.
43. Italicized English word in Novo's original.
44. Novo and his friends, were called *"las chicas de Donceles,"* or "the girls of Maiden Street."
45. Jean Lorrain (1855–1906), a French symbolist famous for his scandalous homosexuality and *décadence,* was born Paul Duval, but changed his name at his father's insistence. "Not born for canonization," he was described by a contemporary.
46. We have a Pope!
47. Italicized English word in Novo's original.
48. Italicized English word in Novo's original.
49. Alberto J. Pani (1878–1955) was an important politician and economist, serving as minister of Industry, Commerce, and Treasury, and of Foreign Relations. A cofounder of the Banco de México, he founded other banks as well, including Crédito Agrícola and BANOBRAS (National Bank for Mortgages and Public Works). His lifelong project was to have Mexico function at an international level of public health, public works, trade, and economics. He wrote an important study on public hygiene as early as 1916, which was a model of its kind.
50. Pedro Henríquez Ureña (1884–1946).
51. Italicized English word in Novo's original.
52. Julio Torri (1889–1970), a poet and essayist; Adolfo ("Fito") Best Maugard (1891–1964), a painter influenced by Aztec art; Jorge Enciso (1879–1969), a painter and author of *Design Motifs of Ancient Mexico.*
53. Italicized English word in Novo's original.
54. Don Derrapadas, the Spanish pseudonym, incorporates both the literal skidding of trucks with the slang for "crazy," "outrageous."
55. Novo's word *cueros,* literally "skins," implies "whores."
56. Italicized English word in Novo's original.
57. The word *toques* is italicized in Novo's original.
58. Ernesto García Cabral (1890–1968), was of Cape Verdean origin, though he was born in Mexico. Nicknamed "Chango" (Monkey), he was one of Mexico's greatest cartoonists, known for his political work and advertising posters for the country's comic films.
59. Luis G. Barreiro (1886–1947), actor, featured in *Prisoner 13, El tigre de Jalisco,* and *El niño perdido,* among many other films.
60. Carlos Luquín, a writer and critic, was part of Teatro Ulises, the experimental

theater group started by Novo and Xavier Villaurrutia.

61. Antonio Caso (1883–1946) was a Mexican essayist and philosopher.

62. Genaro Fernández MacGregor (1883–1959) trained at the Escuela Nacional de Jurisprudencia; taught international public and private law; wrote on literature, art, and law; was an advisor at the Mexican embassy in Washington, D.C.; and served as rector of UNAM (National Autonomous University of Mexico).

"THIS FLOWER OF FOURTEEN PETALS"

1. Novo's quotes are taken from his introduction to *Mil y un sonetos mexicanos* (Mexico City: Editorial Porrúa, 1963), which he edited and introduced.

SONNETS

1. Novo invents the word *endocrinar* (in reference to the endocrine system), so I do likewise, using *endocrinate*. Emphasis should be placed on the second syllable: en**do**crinate.

Index